Just-in-Time
Management

Also by Cy Charney

The Instant Manager: *More than 100 Quick Tips and Techniques for Great Results*

The Instant Sales Pro: *More than 600 Tips and Techniques to Accelerate Your Sales Success*

The Leader's Tool Kit: *Hundreds of Tips and Techniques for Developing the Skills You Need*

The Portable Mentor: *Your Anywhere, Anytime Career Coach and Problem Solver*

The Salesperson's Handbook

The Trainer's Tool Kit

Time to Market: *Reducing Product Lead Time*

Yes You Can! *Reaching Your Potential While Achieving Greatness* (co-author)

Just-in-Time Management

Over 950 Practical Lessons
Your MBA Professor Didn't Teach You

CY CHARNEY

CHARNEY AND ASSOCIATES INC.

Published by Charney and Associates Inc. www.askcharney.com

ISBN 978-0-9731885-5-4

First Published in 2011 by
BPS Books
Toronto and New York
A division of Bastian Publishing Services Ltd.

Cataloguing-in-Publication Data available from Library and Archives Canada.

Cover: Gnibel
Text design and typesetting: Daniel Crack, Kinetics Design kdbooks.ca

Printed by Lightning Source, Tennessee. Lightning Source paper, as used in this book, does not come from endangered old-growth forests or forests of exceptional conservation value. It is acid free, lignin free, and meets all ANSI standards for archival-quality paper. The print-on-demand process used to produce this book protects the environment by printing only the number of copies that are purchased.

This book is dedicated to the thousands of people from organizations around the world who have made my chosen career of management consulting a privilege. I owe most of what I have learned to all of you.

I consider myself very rich by most standards. I have it all. I have good health and an optimistic outlook. I have surrounded myself with wonderful people and have control over my life.

In particular, I am blessed by a special, caring family. My wife, Rhona, counsels people with addictions. Daneal, my eldest daughter, an author in her own right, has a management consulting practice that focuses on Millennials (she is also the source of many of my ideas about managing a new generation of employees). My son-in-law, Dan, is the most professional and caring dentist in town. Thalia, my middle child, practices Naturopathic Medicine. And Davin, my son the lawyer, advocates for all those who are powerless and less able to fend for themselves. Finally, I have two grandchildren, Yael and Limona, who give me regular doses of joy that will ensure I live a happy life until my last day.

I am indeed very rich.

Contents

Preface

I *have written many books*, thinking each one would be the last. But the craziness of recent events has suggested the need for another. Today, storied corporations with the highest of reputations, corporations that have been around for over a century, collapse virtually overnight. This suggests that today's successful managers will need to be quite different from those of the past. They need to have their antennae up, sensing what is happening outside their organization and all around our small world. Today, problems and opportunities are less predictable than in the past. Managers need to be fast of pace, nimble of mind, and swift of foot. Their strategic plans need to be modified and their people's energies galvanized and redirected.

In short, we need managers who are more like cheetahs than elephants.

Being successful in today's environment cannot be reduced to a few habits or principles. As useful as that may be, it is just a start. You, my readers, need a resource that will give just-in-time answers to the ongoing challenges you're faced with daily. I guarantee it: If you use this book as a quick reference guide and put the skills it recommends into practice right away, you will feel and see your competency improve daily. The result will be great working environments, healthy and successful organizations, and splendid managerial careers in today's organizations.

I

How to...
BE AN EFFECTIVE LEADER

Lessons 1–63

How to...
Be an Effective Leader

A boss creates fear, a leader confidence.
A boss fixes blame, a leader corrects mistakes.
A boss knows all, a leader asks questions.
A boss makes work drudgery, a leader makes it interesting.
A boss is interested in himself or herself, a leader is interested
in the group.

– RUSSEL H. EWING

Core competencies is a term that refers to the knowledge, skills, and attitudes that make a significant difference between average and superior performance. Competencies describe in behavioral terms what a high performer looks like in a particular role. They are specific and observable. The competencies of leaders are different from those of managers who require a higher amount of technical ability. But leaders are people with influencing ability – people who are savvy and can get things done by leveraging the talent of those around them.

Here are the top ten competencies that will turn an average performer into a high-performing leader. These constitute the first ten lessons in this book.

1 **Vision**. Vision is the ability to see beyond the turmoil of the day and to create an optimistic picture of possibilities.

2 **Passion**. Only a leader with passion will have the persever-

ance to carry on until the desired outcome is achieved. If you don't have this, your vision will wither and die.

3 Optimism. Optimism is the ability to see the brighter side of things even in the face of setbacks. It is not about ignoring reality; it is the ability to stop thinking and speaking destructively about the circumstances you are in – the ability to see them as temporary. Optimists solve problems effectively. They see solutions where others see only roadblocks.

4 Courage. Organizations are hard to change. Employees hold on to their habitual practices. Without persistent action, little will get done and the changes that do take place will soon revert to the old ways. So leaders of change need to be thick skinned and ready for the hostility and cynicism that will typically be associated with change.

5 Integrity. People will interact with you differently if you can communicate your inner value system and adhere to it. This will produce a respectful environment that values such behaviors as honesty, collaboration, consultation, and transparency.

6 Connection. This is the ability to create a level of psychological intimacy with fellow employees. Tight-knit relationships result in improved morale and increased openness to change. Connection also leads to a sense of community, moving members from a "me" mentality to a "we" mentality.

7 Humility. Humble people enjoy taking a back seat to others and appreciate seeing their subordinates earn the kudos they deserve. They are keenly interested in what others think and feel and enjoy acknowledging those around them. Humble people also know their limits. They surround themselves with people who complement their skills and have no problem deferring to another'sexpertise. They take care to acknowledge the capabilities of the people around them.

8 Caring. Effective leaders have a sense of social responsibility. They are interested in sharing gains with others but keep setbacks to themselves. They are sensitive and willing to respond to the emotional needs of others. They demonstrate an interest and concern for others. Caring, like empathy, is not about being "nice." It is about understanding the positions of others whether you agree with them or not.

9 Driven. Effective leaders are goal oriented. They know when to consult and when to command. When time is of the essence, the direction clear, and all the evidence is in, they expect those around them to follow their lead and go the extra mile.

10 Self-awareness. Everyone has feelings and emotions but few people analyze what causes them and why. People with a high level of self-awareness are able to understand what triggers them to feel irritable, sad, or charming and can see how these behaviors might impact others. This ability is critical to self-development since understanding oneself is the foundation of change.

How to...
Be authentic

Giving people a little more than they expect is a good way to get back more than you'd expect.

– ROBERT HALF

Effective leaders *are sincere and authentic. Authentic people don't try to pretend they are something they're not. They are not phony. Their competence, honesty, and sincerity are evident at all times. They don't need to pretend to be anything other than themselves.*

11 Authentic leaders are completely straightforward. They don't put on airs. They are genuine and sincere and earn respect for who they are rather than who they pretend to be.

12 Authentic leaders are centered in themselves. They feel comfortable with their own values and principles and always feel a sense of completeness in the meaning or purpose of their lives.

13 Authentic people don't lose touch with reality; they have both feet on the ground. They don't fall easily into chronic anxiety, boredom, or despair because they are solidly conscious of their values. Accordingly, when faced with significant challenges, they avoid quick fixes and see little value in anesthetizing themselves with alcohol or drugs to dull the pain of their reality.

14 Inauthentic leaders easily lose the trust of their employees. People are less likely to volunteer ideas or information when their leader's motives are not understood. Instead, they will likely question those motives and give less than a one hundred percent effort. The resulting undercurrents of mistrust sap employee energy. As a consequence, the trust and camaraderie that provide emotional and spiritual fuel go lacking.

15 Why are some leaders inauthentic? It could be because of:

✓ Personality traits. Some people come across as guarded because they are naturally reserved. When such a person is in a formal leadership position, subordinates often feel uncomfortable because they're not sure what their boss is thinking or feeling. Leaders of this personality type should consider ways to reduce the resulting uneasiness in others. Finding ways to communicate more openly and honestly, free of personal agendas, will go a long way toward improving trust and relationships. And communicating more frequently will make a difference too.

✓ Expectations of hierarchical, bureaucratic organizational models. Classic models of bureaucratic behavior promote the belief that, if managers show signs of being genuine and vulnerable, they are weak and ineffectual. Added to that is the belief that managers should have all the answers. Both assumptions create distance. But knowledge is not the single source of power of really effective leaders. Ultimately, leadership is more about who you are than what you know.

16 Inauthentic leaders will try to create a false image. But their people will see straight through it. Everybody is vulnerable. Nobody is perfect or invincible. Nor should we expect our leaders to be like Superman. The more self-confident leaders are, the easier it is for them to be vulnerable. If you are a self-confident leader, people can critique you without fearing that you'll be defensive or may even retaliate.

17 Great leaders are passionate about their organization and its future. Authenticity works hand in hand with passion. You can't project passion effectively without authenticity.

18 Authentic leaders listen to their people. Successful industry leaders have demonstrated that to retain, inspire, mentor, and stretch today's employees, they must hear what those workers are saying. But listening alone is not enough. A leader has to create opportunities and processes to ensure that discussions about the issues of the day can take place in an open spirit, with stakeholders both inside and outside the organization.

19 Authentic leaders are able to listen both to what is being said and what is left unspoken. Being open to new information, no matter how frightening or personally distasteful it may be, gives them the ability to amend their understanding of a changing environment. This openness is demonstrated when leaders

✓ have a good grasp of their organization's capacity
✓ seek new strategies to meet new challenges
✓ are able to abandon cherished ways of acting when new responses are more appropriate
✓ amend their vision based on changing reality

20 Authentic leaders are able to build trust. Trust is the psychological glue that holds employees together. By demonstrating faith in others, a leader sets the example for others to work more openly.

21 Authentic leaders relish opportunities to learn through feedback. Listening to what is being said in the trenches gives leaders the opportunity to move beyond personal expectations of what should be occurring into what is really happening.

How to...
Be humble

To be humble to superiors is duty,
to equals courtesy, to inferiors nobleness.

– BENJAMIN FRANKLIN

A **humble person** *is modest, lacks pretence, and does not believe they are superior to others.*

The biggest surprise Jim Collins encountered in researching his best-selling book From Good to Great *was that humility was the key difference between goodness and greatness. In retrospect, this seems obvious. It surprised Collins, however, because he, like many of us, saw great leaders as being single-minded or charismatic. While these and other traits are important, people place more value on working for someone who is humble. Why?*

22 Humble people are great listeners. While they're typically smart – maybe smarter than most of their employees – they withhold opinions and judgment so they can hear the opinions of others.

23 Humble people don't have to continually hear themselves speak. In meetings, their comments are measured. They contribute only when they are asked or have something significant to offer. And they are always willing to entertain other opinions.

24 Humble people lead from the side by sheer force of example. Their values are known and respected wherever they go. They have little need to elbow others out of the way.

25 Humble people get the job done without drawing attention to themselves. They are patient and content to have their reward come in the long term. By that time, the flaming stars have burned themselves out.

26 Humble people have a wonderful impact on employee morale. Their unpretentiousness galvanizes enthusiasm. It encourages openness in others, boosting self-confidence in others.

27 Humble people are human. And, as such, they make mistakes. But they don't hide them, deny them, or seek to minimize them by pointing out the mistakes of others. Instead, they own up and apologize if necessary.

How to...
Operate from a value system

Effective leaders embody a clear set of values that others appreciate and want to emulate. Many effective leaders would score high in Emotional Intelligence. They embody these important behaviors and values:

28 **Integrity**. Effective leaders honor their commitments. They are honest and don't try to hide flaws in their performance even when they are embarrassed by them.

29 **Fairness**. Leaders need to be fair to everyone. While they can't value everyone the same, they try to treat each person as equally as possible.

30 **Accountability**. Leaders never shirk responsibility. When things go well, they spread the accolades around. But when the going gets tough, they remain to deal with the fallout.

Not only do they accept responsibility for the problem, they accept the responsibility for fixing it.

31 Dependability. Leaders need to be dependable. They must keep their promises and do whatever they can not to let others down.

32 Conscientiousness. Effective leaders work hard. They strive for excellence. They go the extra mile and are always stretching themselves and others to excel.

33 Empathy. Leaders need to have empathy for those around them. They need to be sensitive and intuitive enough to pick up on unspoken problems. When problems do surface, the empathetic leader needs to be able to see the issues from the other's perspective.

34 Composure. Great leaders moderate their emotions. They are not volatile, getting overexcited over small issues or becoming overly upset when problems are raised. They need to make tough decisions based on facts, not emotions.

35 Optimism. Leaders need to remember that dark clouds will pass. It is up to them to project the sense that the future is friendly and remind others that the sun will soon be shining again. Optimistic people see solutions where other people see problems.

36 Generosity. Admired leaders are generous. They are charitable to any and all worthy causes and seldom withhold their time – their most precious commodity – or their resources. And, when they give, they do so with an open heart. Giving anonymously, which is difficult for most of us, comes more easily to them.

37 Appreciation. Effective leaders show appreciation for the contribution of others. Giving formal and informal praise comes easily to them.

How to...
Create an ethical environment

Radical changes in world politics leave America with a heightened responsibility to be, for the world, an example of a genuinely free, democratic, just and humane society.

– POPE JOHN PAUL II

People **look to leaders** to model appropriate behavior for them. High on the list is ethical behavior.

Getting your head around ethics is like understanding good parenting – you know it's desirable and worth the effort, but it's hard to pin down.

There is always a great temptation to consider only the short term and to cut corners and operate profitably at the expense of ethics. The tendency to offer more benefits and favors to those closest to us (cronyism) is also powerful. Here are some guidelines for ethical behavior:

38 Understand that there are different types of ethical behavior:

✓ *Personal Ethics*
These are the principles that conscientious parents have tried to instill in us. They include:
- concern for others
- respect for the autonomy of others

- honesty
- trustworthiness
- fairness
- benevolence
- prevention of harm
- sharing

✓ *Professional Ethics*

Many professions have a formal code of conduct that, if broken, could lead to censure or even expulsion. They include such concerns as
- impartiality
- openness and full disclosure
- confidentiality
- due diligence
- avoidance of conflict of interest

✓ *Global Ethics*

Ethical principles are especially challenging for corporations that operate across borders. They include
- respect for international and local laws
- social responsibility
- a holistic approach
- environmental stewardship

39 Make ethical behavior a priority. Promote ethical actions in as many ways as possible.

✓ Define and document your company's ethical principles. Involve all stakeholders in this process. Share these principles with everyone, ensuring that they are available and easy to access. For example, they should be part of orientation for new employees, in the employees' handbook, on your Web page, and posted in offices and meeting rooms.

✓ Set up an ethics committee under a respected ombudsperson from outside the corporation to deal with grievances and conflicts.

✓ Perform regular (annual) audits of corporate behaviors and compare the results with the documented ideal. Analyze the results, look for gaps, and develop plans for improvement. Make sure that the process is open.

✓ Train and orient all employees on how to implement the defined codes of ethics and behavior.

40 Include ethical behavior in performance reviews.

41 Define consequences for those who do not operate according to the established principles.

42 Empower and encourage employees to "blow the whistle" any time behaviors, products, or services clearly contravene corporate standards.

43 Include ethical behavior when judging new recruits on their abilities.

44 Include ethical behavior as a criterion in decisions regarding promotions.

45 Conduct regular verifications to ensure that claims made for products and services are accurate and true.

46 Encourage your company's board of directors to approve systems that ensure compliance with the code of ethics.

47 Involve the board in periodic reviews and fine-tuning of the code of ethics.

48 Build ethical standards into your dealings with the outside world, especially your customers.

✓ Always promise realistic results. When providing a service, be reasonable about expectations, and remember that the best results tend to come from long-term, sustained efforts.

✓ Don't look to make a quick killing in a situation where the buyer is somewhat naïve. Sooner or later the truth will come out; the consequences will inevitably come back to haunt you later on.

How to...
Build a new generation of leaders

Leadership is the ability to develop leaders not followers.

– Peter Block

*W*orking with the youth *of any generation can be a challenging task. In the not too distant future, your organization will have a high percentage of Generation Y'ers: those born between 1981 and 1999. Men and women from these ranks will be tasked to carry your company into the future and take responsibility for its success. Leaders need to learn more about this generation and its values, needs, and expectations so they can encourage them to stay and contribute. At present, most leave after only two years, just when they're up to speed and ready to contribute in a meaningful way.*

The following strategies will make a difference in developing these new entrants to the workplace.

49 Identify the best candidates. Finding the right criteria for this identification will not be easy. Solid Generation Y candidates will most likely be a work-in-progress. They are still relatively new to their careers, so we have much to learn about them in the workforce. Here are some ways to bring the highest-caliber talent into your organization:

   ✓ Interview as many candidates as possible. You'll need to

gather as much information as possible on this generation while trying to understand them.

✓ Don't judge a book by its cover. Remember that this generation's upbringing may be unfamiliar to you. Look for accomplishments, versus just education and work experience, on a résumé.

✓ Invite candidates to conduct part of the interview. We know this generation is very outspoken and not afraid to ask for what they want. You can assess motivation and intellect as early as the interview stage if it is conducted correctly. Remember that their mentality is just as much "what can you do for me" as "what can I do for you."

✓ Seek them out through non-traditional means. Using networking tools (mainly online) is important for two reasons: speed and range. You'll reach the most people in the shortest time by posting ads or information on popular Internet sites.

✓ Give them a chance to "show their stuff" as a part of the interview process. For example, have them do some programming or make a presentation. You'll learn a lot about their attitudes and abilities when they are challenged.

50 Attract younger employees through non-traditional means. This will be a challenge because they will often be the ones selecting you. Once hired, you will be challenged to retain these high-expectation employees.

✓ Embrace all online networking tools. Many companies have banned sites like Myspace and Facebook, but the Website itself is not the issue; the performance of the employee is. If you want to keep Generation Y interested, allow them the freedom to use the tools they grew up with. But hold them accountable for their performance.

✓ Provide flexible compensation packages. Money is still a

motivator for this generation, but balancing work with leisure carries much more weight than in times past. By offering options weighted for salary or vacation time, you will attract the best and the brightest.

✓ Keep your technology as current as possible. There are things you can do to keep things current without breaking the bank. Hardware and software can be expensive, but little changes can make a big difference. For example, if your company sponsors cell phones or PDA's, simply updating the devices every year will keep things fresh for your employees. You may even be able to have the supplier absorb the costs by negotiating a long-term contract.

51 Develop your younger employees.

✓ Engage them in projects early. Getting them into teams with goals and time lines will give you a good indication of their commitment, while satisfying their need to be involved right away.

✓ Ensure that they are involved in projects on top of their regular work duties. Multi-tasking comes more easily to this generation; it may be a disadvantage to you and them if they are focused only on one task. The idle hands of an experienced multi-tasker can be the devil's workshop.

✓ Pair them with a mentor. Give them someone who can show them the ropes and guide them in a way that helps them avoid the faux pas that could negatively impact their image with peers and managers. Selecting a mentor can be tough, but usually an open-minded Baby Boomer, or Generation X colleague should do the trick. Generation Y'ers are very collaborative; they should work well in a team.

✓ Be prepared for direct feedback – even encourage it. Generation Y staff will speak their minds and will be blunt. It would be wise to interpret the meaning of their message instead of focusing on the words spoken. If understood correctly, direct communication can often be used to your advantage: You may hear things your other staff don't have the courage to tell you.

✓ Give feedback, both positive and/or constructive, to them as often as possible. This is your tool to help them calibrate their work. Because it's what they crave, you will be respected for it. It should also open the doors to solid, two-way dialogue and trust. This will assist you in understanding what they really want and how they really think.

✓ Point them in the right direction and give them space to innovate. This generation has been taught to network ever since the first computer was hooked up to the Internet. They're built for networking. Give them guidance and watch what unfolds.

How to...
Be effective every day

Productivity is never an accident.
It is always the result of a commitment to excellence,
intelligent planning, and focused effort.

– PAUL J. MEYER

Employees are always looking to you, their leader, as a role model to be emulated. Your behavior will be copied by some and decried by others. Employees will also be critical of your actions if these do not mesh with your words or with the purported values and principles of the organization.

Here are some ideas for increasing your effectiveness and credibility.

52 Operate daily in a way that would make your mother proud. If you're not sure whether a behavior or action is appropriate, ask yourself, "What would my mother say?"

53 Always be prepared. Whenever you go to a meeting, demonstrate that you are on top of things. Be sure to read the previous meeting's minutes and have your report ready to present. Demonstrate a passion for excellence and expect the same from others.

54 Maintain a focus for your actions. Spend most of your time adding value to stakeholders. Demonstrate a passion for client/customer service. Under promise and over deliver. Always try to delight those you serve.

55 Build alliances. You can never have enough friends. Think about those who could bring you down and reach out to them. Demonstrate your good faith by complimenting them publicly whenever appropriate. Thank them in private if you see a change in their approach to you. And don't bad-mouth them indiscriminately behind their backs, what you say is sure to come back to haunt you.

56 Become a lifelong learner. Treat each day as an opportunity to gain new information. Learn from your mistakes. Read everything that excites you and ask lots of questions of people whose skills are complementary to yours. Take time each year to take in a workshop that will give you leading-edge information. And take at least one course that will take you out of your comfort zone but could give you an interesting new avenue of development. Debrief with every member of your staff who has attended a course to find out what they learned.

57 Manage differences professionally. There are always differences of opinion. Focus on the issue and not the person. Listen empathetically to make sure you understand the other's position and treat it as a legitimate concern. Look for items of mutual agreement before dealing with differences. Always maintain a calm composure when differences are raised. Maintain a firm and collaborative voice and body language as you become assertive in making your opinions known.

58 Be truthful. Don't exaggerate or quote numbers as if they were facts when they're only your opinion. And don't lie when you know something is not true. Even white lies can come back to bite you and destroy the trust you have taken so much time to build.

How to...
Groom your successor

No one can go it alone. Somewhere along the line is the person who gives you faith that you can make it.

– GRACE GIL OLIVERA

You're **not going to be promoted** *if you can't be replaced. That's why grooming your replacement (a protégé) is important. However, because many organizations have downsized to the point where employees are working to full capacity, finding time to develop new skills can be a challenge. This means the pool of suitable replacements is shallow, resulting in people being promoted for their potential rather than their ability. With these challenges in mind, here are some ways you can make sure you're ready to be replaced seamlessly when the call comes.*

59 See yourself as a coach. Make it your business to identify one or two high-potential employees for development. Create a plan that will enable them to step into your shoes at any time.

60 Review the skills that made you successful: organizational, technical, and "soft" skills. Evaluate potential replacements and identify gaps in their abilities. Let them know about your intention to develop them as your backup – this will be highly motivating for them.

61 Identify your replacement's learning style. Some people are more self-directed while others prefer more structure, help, and guidance as they learn. Those who are more self-directed and able to take responsibility for their career and learning are probably going to be better replacements. Prioritize topics with your protégé, and develop a list of learning opportunities (conferences, workshops, mentoring, readings, and challenging assignments, to name a few) they will be given over a reasonable period of time.

62 Encourage retention of new skills by setting goals before each learning opportunity. Equally important, follow up to find out how effective the training was, what was learned, and what new skills or behavior you can expect. Reinforce the learning as often as you can; research indicates that for learning to be internalized it needs to be reinforced five to six times.

63 Challenge your protégé with work assignments. On-the-job learning can be powerful. Ensure that each assignment has four phases:

✓ *Planning.* Identify the goals of the assignment. Next, specify what steps (actions) are expected and what the final outcome (deliverables) is to be. Involve the protégé in the plan to ensure that they buy into the goals you are setting.

✓ *Action.* Allow the protégé to carry out the project. Monitor their progress, offering encouragement along the way. Note how they deal with adversity. Do they look to you for help when they encounter a roadblock or do they find a way to overcome the obstacle themselves? Identify key points along the way to evaluate progress so you can give them helpful feedback.

✓ *Evaluation.* Make notes on your observations so you can be specific in your feedback. Also, if possible, measure progress so your feedback will be specific rather than general. Having pointed out any shortcomings that you may have observed, get your protégé's agreement on the facts presented. Then ask them to suggest new strategies to deal with the situation. You should suggest solutions only if they have no idea how to deal with the situation in the future (which is highly unlikely).

✓ *Revision.* Create a new plan for learning something new or set up a similar project to perfect your protégé's learning.

II

How to...
BE PRODUCTIVE

Lessons 64–141

How to...
Make your meetings effective (and short!)

[Football] combines the two worst things about American life. It is violent, punctuated by a committee meeting.

– GEORGE WILL

***B**ad meetings are the bane* of every manager's existence and the butt of corporate jokes. Still, for a team or a project to run smoothly, participants have to meet to get updated, pool ideas, compare notes, plan, make decisions, and build cohesion. Following are some simple practices that will increase the effectiveness of your meetings.

Before Meetings

64 Ask yourself whether a meeting is really needed. Is there a quicker and better way to achieve your purpose? In fact, is there even a clear goal for the meeting? Bear in mind that time spent in meetings is time spent away from working on the project. If there is a more efficient way to exchange ideas and data, use it.

65 Invite only the people who need to be there. Stragglers will simply be bored and negatively impact the tone of the meeting.

66 Keep it simple. Focus on a few items only. Overloading the agenda will result in many more action items, a good number of which will probably not get done.

67 Prepare. Create a time-based agenda beforehand. Send the agenda and other necessary documents to participants beforehand to allow them to prepare. And book the meeting room well in advance.

68 Get to the meeting room early to ensure that it's set up the way you like and that all equipment is functioning.

At the Meeting

69 Start the meeting right: Get agreements from the participants regarding the objective, time, and process (method to deal with each agenda item).

70 Establish ground rules in advance, especially if the participants don't know each other well, and get their buy-in. These may include items such as:

✓ listening to each other
✓ respecting each other
✓ turning off electronic devices
✓ volunteering to take action items as may be appropriate
✓ sticking to the agenda
✓ focusing on issues, not people

71 Get organized. Involve team members in different roles. Assign one person to keep minutes, another to keep time, a third to record key ideas on a flip chart when necessary, and a fourth to make sure the ground rules are observed.

72 Work through the agenda item by item, keeping to the schedule but dealing with each item before moving on. Stay on track and encourage others to do so. If items come up that are not on the agenda, thank the individual concerned and suggest that they be dealt with at the end of the meeting, time permitting, or at the next meeting. Or, if the items are not relevant to others at the meeting, briefly discuss how they may be dealt with offline.

73 If relevant materials were not passed out beforehand, distribute them when the item comes up so you don't distract the participants.

74 Focus on the process. If you're using Robert's Rules, ensure that everyone is heard and that motions are adopted and passed according to the rules. Allow participants to contribute to the content.

75 If you're not using a formal process, focus on the process and behave in a neutral and impartial manner whenever possible. Other than when you are providing information, you should be listening intently, asking questions, getting agreement, and summarizing as required. Questions to ask include:

✓ What's next on the agenda?
✓ How does everyone feel about this?
✓ Are there any other opinions about this?
✓ How much time do we have left?
✓ How will we deal with this issue?
✓ Should we take a vote?
✓ Can everyone live with that?
✓ Are we done?

76 Involve everybody. Don't let one or two people (including you) dominate the discussion.

77 Where possible and when appropriate, reach decisions by consensus. Make sure no one interrupts, talks over others, or intimidates anyone else.

78 Summarize each decision to make sure that there is a clear action item, that responsibility has been assigned, and that a completion date has been agreed to.

79 Thank everyone for attending and compliment them if the meeting has been productive. If not, ask them what you could have done better to make the meeting more effective. If this is difficult to do publicly, approach people who are likely to be objective and solicit their feedback.

After the Meeting

80 Send the minutes to participants and post them on the department bulletin board. Highlight each participant's commitment on their copy of the minutes.

How to...
Keep things simple and speed things up

At times it is necessary to go over the top.
How else can we get to the other side?

– *Kobi Yamada*

*A*ll the steps we take to deliver *a product or service to a client (internal or external) are known as processes. Studies of work processes suggest that the value-added steps (of benefit to clients) in a process typically consume only five percent of the total time. This means that ninety-five percent of the time there are no value-added activities and the process has ground to a halt. So the opportunity to reduce time spent getting things done properly is enormous. In addition, most processes are unpredictable.*

Sometimes they are quick, sometimes slow. Sometimes they are correct, and sometimes not. Sometimes we are treated well, and sometimes abruptly. The unacceptable delays and lack of predictability need to change – the opportunity to do better is huge.

Here's how you can work with your people to radically improve process:

Step 1: Identify an opportunity

81 Find a process that can be improved. This will not be difficult

– they all can be improved! Where do you start? Prioritize the opportunities by asking:

✓ Is it causing a lot of customer complaints?

✓ If it could be shortened, improved, or made more predictable, would it save us significant funds?

✓ Would its improvement have an impact on the achievement of our mission?

✓ Is it relatively simple to solve?

✓ Would senior management be delighted with the change?

This analysis will help you identify which process to work on first.

Step 2: Form a team to work on the opportunity

82 Invite six to ten people to help you improve the process. The team should represent all aspects of the process and include personnel from each department to contribute to the final deliverable. Look for volunteers who:

✓ understand the process
✓ are anxious to improve it
✓ have some hands-on experience with it
✓ will make time to work on the project
✓ have the power to make changes (at least one)
   • If your team consists of front-line people, you will need a mandate from a senior manager to make changes. Such a mandate will give participants confidence that their hard work will not be in vain.

83 Hold your first team meeting. At the kickoff you should:

✓ Introduce members to one another.
✓ Explain the process and steps you will be taking.
✓ Train people in the tools of process mapping.
✓ Get commitments from each person regarding their participation and contribution.

Step 3: Map the process

84 Give people a week to collect information about the process and list the steps that take place in their team/department.

85 At your next meeting, record all the steps of the process on a whiteboard. The board should be pre-drawn with the people/departments involved listed on the left vertical axis and a time line on the horizontal (bottom) axis.

86 Record each step in the process on separate Post-it™ notes. Record activities, starting on the left side and moving to the right. The advantage of using these notes is that they can be easily moved and changed. If you are unsure about any part of the map, leave it blank and continue. You can do detailed research later.

87 Use appropriate symbols for each step in the process. The most commonly used icons are:

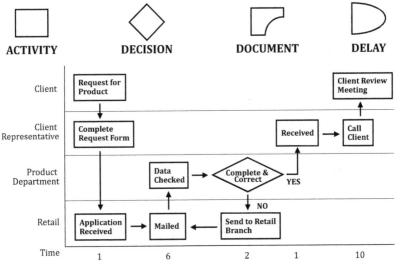

Diagram 1: Example of a simple process map

✓ The process map should show
  • each step

- the inputs and outputs of each step
- all decisions
- the people involved
- the time to do each step

✓ Make a draft of the process and give team members the opportunity to confirm its accuracy with their peers.

Step 4: Analyze the process

88 At your next meeting, adjust the process based on feedback from team members.

89 Benchmark your process to determine just how effective it is. Compare it to others who are more effective than you. If it is completely ineffective, consider scrapping it. If it requires fine-tuning, analyze it step-by-step.

90 Analyze the process by determining whether:
✓ each step is necessary
✓ the flow is logical
✓ each step adds value
✓ any steps are missing
✓ any steps are wasteful
✓ there is duplication of effort

91 List the problems. Prioritize them based on their impact on the customer, their cost, and the effort required to fix them.

92 Taking one problem at a time, find the major cause(s). These are typically people, methods, materials, or machinery (equipment).

✓ Solve the major problems' cause(s).

Step 5: Redesign the process

93 Based on the team's ideas, redraw the process map to reduce waste, duplication, and time.

Step 6: Implement change

94 Develop action plans for all the improvements. Spread the changes among as many people as possible so the workload is evenly distributed.

95 Hold meetings with all those affected to make sure they:
- ✓ understand the changes
- ✓ agree to the changes
- ✓ will make the changes

Step 7: Monitor and hold gains

96 Follow up with people to make sure the changes are being implemented.

97 Encourage and recognize efforts to reduce the difficulties usually associated with change.

Step 8: Measure the results

98 Keep a tally of the improvements. Charting them and displaying them for everyone to see will promote pride and a sense of accomplishment among all those involved in the project. It will also increase enthusiasm for your next process-improvement project.

How to...
Improve productivity

Most people like hard work,
particularly when they're paying for it.

– FRANKLIN P. JONES

Productivity – *the efficiency with which we produce goods or services – is a critical component of being competitive. Productivity gives us the flexibility to reduce costs and expand profit margins. Or it will allow us to reduce costs in the expectation of selling more. Here are some ideas that will spur you to improve:*

99 Determine how you and your associates spend time. Ask yourself what percentage of the time available you spend doing activities directly related to your objectives and client-related activities. Anything less than ninety percent suggests a problem.

100 Have clear objectives for the department, team, and individuals. Share these with your employees so everyone knows and understands the target. Improve ownership and buy-in by involving employees in setting the goals and coming up with plans for improvement.

101 Encourage employees to focus on their goals by setting and monitoring mini-goals. That's how you can track whether there is progress and whether an employee needs to be redirected before time is lost.

102 Measure the team's progress toward its objectives. Record these and post them so people can see changes. Review them at all meetings. Be sure to give appropriate recognition for achievements.

103 If objectives are not achieved, hold a meeting with staff to find the cause of the problem. Be careful to avoid finger pointing. Look for creative solutions to the problem and create an action plan to address the issues.

104 Encourage associates to measure their own productivity so they feel responsibility for their own performance.

105 Listen to and implement new ideas that enable you and your employees to work smarter, not harder. Encourage and reward associates for trying new ideas.

106 Give recognition for suggestions. Share new ideas with others in your team so they can benefit too.

107 Evaluate key processes regularly. Involve your people in documenting all steps in their process and constantly agree on refinements that eliminate waste, duplication, and delays.

108 Focus on doing jobs right the first time. Doing things in a hurry will lead to mistakes that result in poor customer service and lower productivity.

109 Involve experts – internal or external – in finding the best way to do a job. Document best practices. Then train your people to follow the revised method so it is performed, consistently, better than before.

110 Cross-train people so they can help one another when work piles up at one workstation. Flexible workers can also fill in for others during breaks, vacations, and sick leaves.

111 Don't automate for the sake of automation. Make the manual process as simple and efficient as possible before considering replacing it with a machine or electronic device.

112 Cut out unnecessary meetings. Hold informal meetings that last no more than five to ten minutes in the office or on the shop floor.

113 Evaluate the necessity of the paperwork you do. Ask yourself:

✓ Does anybody read it?
✓ Does anyone care about the information?
✓ Does the content lead to decisions?

If the answer to any of these questions is no, fight to simplify or eliminate the report.

114 Organize the work area. Put things where they are clearly visible or can be found easily. Searching for documents can take up to thirty percent of people's time.

115 Review the sequence of activities in your work area. Move people to promote an even and effective flow. Also, move people who work well with each other closer together to improve communications and reduce excessive handling.

116 Document the steps of your work processes, starting with the one that causes the most complaints. When the process is described in detail, have the team responsible for it meet to ask themselves these tough questions:

✓ Is each step in our process necessary?
✓ Does each step add value for our customers?
✓ Are some steps duplicated?
✓ Can any steps be removed?
✓ Can we automate any steps?

✓ Are some activities missing?

✓ Who is responsible for quality? The associate, manager, or someone in quality control?

✓ Do people check their own work or is it left to someone else to do at completion?

✓ Is the work-flow logical?

✓ Are related activities positioned next to each other?

✓ Do we have policies and procedures that prevent improvements?

✓ Do people have the power to make improvements in their own jobs?

✓ Do we measure productivity?

✓ Do we share productivity data with our associates?

✓ Have we involved our associates in suggesting productivity improvements?

✓ Do we have unnecessary levels of approval?

✓ Where does the process stop for the longest time? Why?

✓ Where are the bottlenecks? How can they be removed?

117 Don't hire more people at peak periods. Get temporary staff. Better still, review procedures to see what can be simplified or eliminated.

118 Benchmark your processes. Benchmarking will enable you to compare your processes with those of acknowledged leaders.

✓ You can benchmark
  • measurable indicators of performance
  • methods and procedures

✓ You can compare the things you do with
  • similar work areas in your organization
  • similar work areas in other organizations
  • different work areas in other organizations

✓ The more willing you are to compare yourself with different organizations, the more likely you will be to find radically new and creative alternative strategies. For example, comparing line-up times at your hydro payment receipts office with those at a hotel check-in desk will reveal more opportunities than comparing them with line-up times at another hydro office.

✓ Modify good ideas from other organizations so they fit your own circumstances.

How to...
Manage your time

Time is nature's way of keeping
everything from happening at once.

– ANONYMOUS

*T*here is only so much time in the day. *Managing it effectively will enable you to balance work and personal life. It will reduce stress and improve your health. Above all, it will improve your career since you will spend more time satisfying your internal and external customers.*

Time is a precious commodity because it is a nonrenewable resource. It can never be recovered, so needs to be used wisely. In addition, time wastage causes unnecessary stress. It can lead to missed deadlines and can result in poor client service. Following are some practical ideas for managing your time more effectively.

Getting Started

119 Visit your office over a weekend and clean house.

  ✓ Throw away miscellaneous pieces of paper such as Post-it™ notes that no longer have a value. Record and store important information electronically.

  • Record all your information in one system.
  • Improve your filing system.
  • Put information where you can access it quickly and easily.

120 Analyze how you spend your time. Use labels. For example: A for time spent serving customers (internal or external); B for time spent on tasks helping someone who is helping a customer; C for time spent on activities that do not benefit customers directly or indirectly (often fun). Record your time spent doing A, B, and C activities over a couple of typical days. Categorize the time. Analyze how much of your time was wasted and make note of the circumstances under which this occurred.

121 Develop a plan to reduce B activities. Write down the plan. Commit to implementation. Consult the plan often.

122 Plan the occasional C activities. Having fun and doing the things you enjoy will help you preserve your sanity! But don't get too caught up in those activities lest they interfere with the A items.

123 Invest in a time management system that will allow you to keep all your notes, reminders, calendar, and directory all together. A small hand-held device that can be updated daily and reconciled with your computer is ideal.

Daily

124 Start each day with a list of all the activities you wish to accomplish.

125 Next, categorize and prioritize each activity as A or B activities. A activities are those that, if not done, will either adversely affect your reputation or negatively impact your service to clients. Any others are B's.

126 Plan to do all A activities first. However, avoid committing more than seventy percent of your day to these activities since unforeseen issues will invariably upset your plans and use up available time.

127 Allocate B items to other dates in your calendar, not necessarily the next day.

128 Keep your daily checklist handy at all times. The list will have little value if you are always looking for it.

129 Keep your desk clean. Put things where you can find them.

130 Use your travel time effectively. Most planes and trains now have phones; cell phones can get reception almost anywhere; and text messaging is easy and cheap. Using your laptop or tablet with few interruptions will help the time fly by.

131 Use your spare time to educate yourself, whether by listening to audiotapes or DVDs in the car or on your iPod when you're having breakfast or walking the dog. Challenge yourself to write down the highlights of what you have learned – while you are enjoying your first morning coffee – this will improve your retention significantly.

132 Avoid meetings that are not critical. If your sole purpose for going to a meeting is to get information, get it from the minutes instead.

133 Delegate your routine work to associates so you can tackle planning, problems, and challenging tasks.

134 Do only one thing at a time and complete it before taking on the next task.

135 Get those you work with to respect your quiet time – the time when you are planning your day's activities (first hour) or cleaning your desk at the end of the day.

136 Avoid procrastination. Identify and deal with the source of your discomfort. The longer you procrastinate, the higher your stress will rise.

137 Do less pleasant but important items first. You will gain a sense of relief and achievement.

138 Monitor your progress. If you feel you're doing better, reward yourself in some way. It's important for your effort to be appreciated even if only by you!

Paperwork

139 Keep your desk clean. Put things where you can find them. Don't put documents in temporary places.

140 Deal with each piece of paper once. File it, respond to it, or dump it.

141 Reduce time by responding to correspondence by writing on it and faxing it back, or by photocopying it and sending it back to the sender.

III

How to...
INCREASE YOUR INFLUENCE

Lessons 142–198

How to...
Become more assertive

*To know how to refuse is as important
as to know how to consent.*

– BALTASAR GRACIAN

Assertiveness is confidence translated into action. It is neither bullying nor browbeating; it is simply allowing your convictions to carry the conversation. Honesty, combined with a non-confrontational manner, is assertiveness, one of the most valuable tools in your managerial kit.

142 Evaluate your level of assertiveness. Ask yourself, do I

- ✓ apologize when I don't have an instant solution to a problem?
- ✓ frequently apologize for my decisions?
- ✓ feel I don't have the right to change my mind?
- ✓ feel guilty when I make mistakes, even when they can be fixed?
- ✓ automatically say yes when someone makes a request?
- ✓ feel foolish asking questions when I don't understand something?
- ✓ follow instructions without question?
- ✓ think my opinion doesn't count, especially if it differs from the majority?
- ✓ feel I don't have the right to ask people to change their behavior toward me?

✓ feel guilty delegating or deferring tasks?
✓ have trouble walking away from an argument?

143 If your answer is yes to most of these questions, then read on! If you have answered no then read this chapter anyway, to confirm your assertive behavior.

To Be More Assertive:

144 Project confident body language. Actors know that physical actions and expressions of an emotion lead them to an actual experience of the emotion.

✓ Lean toward the person you're trying to influence.
✓ Get into their space.
✓ Don't slouch.
✓ Make and maintain eye contact (if this makes you nervous at first, stare at the bridge of the person's nose until you feel comfortable meeting their gaze).
✓ If you sit, place your hands on the table and don't fidget. If you stand, don't pace. Stillness projects confidence.

145 Speak with authority. Assertive people enunciate, allowing each carefully articulated point to make an impact on their audience before they move on. Speak clearly, and always address someone in particular, rather than the air.

146 Take ownership of issues. Make it yours by using "I" statements. Couple this with letting people know how you feel about the issues ("I feel upset.") Stick to the point and end on a strong note; don't dwindle off, saying "and so on" or "et cetera."

147 Confirm understandings. Build commitment to action by constantly confirming agreements to your point of view ("Can you see why I'm upset?" or "Do you agree that this is an issue of concern?")

148 Present your idea with confidence.

149 Don't be afraid to defend the processes you've set out. Don't feel guilty about saying no. However, if someone offers a real improvement to your plan, incorporate it. That person is not showing you up – they are helping your overall plan succeed. Being assertive does not mean being stubborn.

150 Focus. Don't get sidetracked. If you feel the conversation is going around in circles, say so and re-state your concern. You may sound like a broken record, but you will get the discussion back on track.

151 Confine the discussion to specific facts and have supporting documentation at hand. Don't use words such as "perhaps" or "maybe." They show uncertainty.

152 Don't generalize about issues. Assertiveness involves solving individual problems to your satisfaction, not making generalized accusations about a subordinate's incompetence. If a letter has a typo, say so. Don't say that someone can't spell. Be confident that the problem can be solved and you will inspire the confidence to get it solved.

153 Maintain your authority. Never begin with an apology or an accusation. A position of authority carries certain rights and responsibilities. The key to being assertive is finding the proper balance between them. You are neither the Tooth Fairy nor the Grim Reaper. Don't use your position of authority to silence the other person prematurely, but don't keep the discussion going long after it's clear no resolution will be reached. If you must agree to disagree, then do so.

How to...
Sell your ideas

A single idea can transform a life,
a team, a business, a nation, a world.

– ANONYMOUS

No matter what their rank, *people in your workplace are dependent on each other. Every day we need to influence our peers, bosses, and subordinates and they influence us. Often this requires change in others and there is often resistance to change. The goal is to influence them to embrace your ideas so a constructive outcome is achieved. These strategies will promote win-win outcomes.*

154 Develop a cooperative and team-oriented outlook. Model the behavior yourself so others will follow suit. Let them know that their actions, when cooperative, are noticed and appreciated.

155 Don't pull rank. Those above you will be resentful and will try to block you and your ideas.

156 Treat people with respect. The better your behavior toward them, the more they'll want to support you and your ideas.

157 Find out what motivates the members of your team and use it to enhance the performance of the team as a whole.

158 Address differences with your peers and subordinates directly – don't appeal to those above you or discuss their intransigence with others. Constructive, empathetic discussions will build trust and strong relationships and help you be more influential in the longer run.

159 Deploy your unique resources for others so they know you are going above and beyond for them. In return, find out what special talents and resources they may have that you can call on at some later stage.

160 Learn to use your powers of persuasion to improve your chances of getting other people to agree. Maximize your power by using a combination of:

✓ **Legitimacy**. Present ideas that are backed up with supporting evidence from credible sources including expert views in books, magazines, and newspaper articles. Present the ideas verbally and in documented form, whether in the form of a report or presentation (PowerPoint™) or both.

✓ **Precedent**. Identify other successes with parallels to your own. If your idea has worked in the past under similar circumstances, mention it. Point to successful pilot projects.

✓ **Facts**. Gather buy-in individually from as many people as possible before generalizing an idea, and collect evidence to demonstrate their support.

✓ **Expertise**. Demonstrate that you are an expert in your field – your knowledge will add to your influence. Or bring in a recognized expert to add legitimacy to the idea.

✓ **Rank**. Get your bosses' input on your idea. If they feel they have contributed to the idea, they will have a sense of ownership; thus their positive opinions will carry extra influence.

✓ **Passion**. Your enthusiasm will impress those around you to take a second look at your idea.

✓ **Persistence**. Don't give up on a great idea; your tenacity will ultimately wear down opposition.

161 Power is only half of the equation in overcoming resistance. The other half relates to relationships. If you have cordial, even warm relationships with others, you will be much more likely to get them to change their minds. Maximizing power is more of a conscious, logical, and cerebral strategy. Developing relationships to promote agreements will require you to:

✓ be patient with people. Listen to their comments and feelings. Don't ignore their non-verbal sentiments.

✓ show that you're listening, understanding, and empathizing. Feed back what you hear and feel. Be clear about what it is they need and try your best to meet their needs. This will increase your chances of having your needs met. Consider trading benefits: "So if I can do that for you, can I expect that you do this for me?"

✓ agree to points you can live with. This reduces tension and turns the conversation into more of a discussion than an argument.

✓ start any rebuttal sentences using the word "and" instead of "but." Say, "I hear what you're saying. And there may be another way of looking at it. Can I share that with you?" This is also a humble approach, and humility is a wonderful way of winning people over.

✓ try to meet their needs by agreeing to something. "Yes, I understand where you're coming from," or "I see what you mean..."

✓ build on agreement. Keep repeating and summarizing so the agreements are cumulative. Say, "So let me be sure I understand our discussion. I see we have agreed to the following..." The greater the number of small agreements you achieve, the higher the probability that you will achieve final agreement.

As Calvin Coolidge put it:

> *Keep believing.*

> *Keep trying.*

> *Persistence and determination alone are omnipotent.*

How to...
Make ideas compelling

Nothing can take the place of persistence.
Talent will not; nothing is more common
than unsuccessful men with talent.
Genius will not; unrewarded genius is a proverb.
Education will not; the world is full of educated derelicts.

– *Calvin Coolidge*

*W**hat's the point** in having great ideas if you can't sell them to the people who control their implementation? And if you never see your idea implemented, how much satisfaction will you derive from it? Here are some ideas to increase your odds of getting approval for your project.*

162 Before you meet with a potential sponsor, be prepared.

- ✓ Pick your best ideas. Don't try to sell every one. Choose those that
  - are aligned with the organization's mission
  - have a reasonable chance of being accepted
  - are the ones you feel passionately about

- ✓ Collect as much information as possible to support your position. Facts speak louder than words.
  - Find examples of where a similar idea might have worked elsewhere. This will enable you to demonstrate a precedent.
  - Don't rely on presenting your ideas orally. Collect

them and put them in documented form. This will add legitimacy to your position. Color brochures of the equipment you want to buy, or expert endorsements in credible trade or business magazines, will enhance your position.

- Make people aware of the possibility that a competitor may use your idea. This sense of rivalry may spur your sponsor to action in hopes of staying one step ahead.
- Be prepared to talk the language of your audience. If you are dealing with management, are you ready to show a cost/benefit? Can you prove, to human resource people, a measurable benefit to morale?

163 When you're making your pitch:

✓ Greet people warmly. Thank them for their time.
  - Let them know your expected outcome. Be specific and assertive. Speak in a firm voice and emphasize key results.
  - Be positive. Saying "I expect to come away from this meeting with approval to start a pilot project" is better than "I hope you'll like my idea . . . perhaps, maybe, you'll let me try it."
  - Don't exaggerate the benefits. Be optimistic yet realistic.
  - Give them a chance to ask questions. Listen carefully to what they have to say. Answer them or offer to get back to them if the answer requires further thought or research.
  - When your presentation is done, be silent. Wait till you get a "buying signal," such as, "When can we start?" or "Do you think we can manage, given our lack of time?" Then assure them of success and show them your timetable.
  - Don't ask for approval in a format they can say no to. Replace "can we go ahead?" with "do you have any other ideas that would ensure success?" or "when do you think we should start?" or "when would you like the project to be completed by?"

164 Study people your whole life. The more you understand about them the more you'll realize how complex and different they are. Learn to adjust your style of "selling" to different personalities.

165 A useful (though oversimplified) model of personality classification comes from Carl Jung, who believed that every person is predominantly one of these four types:

✓ feeling
✓ thinking
✓ intuitive
✓ sensing

166 **Feeling people** make decisions based on people. You will notice they:

✓ enjoy chitchat
✓ are as interested in you as in what service or product you offer
✓ need to see a human value to their purchase
✓ need to feel comfortable with you before reviewing what you have to offer

You can spot a feeler by noticing

✓ items of a personal nature in their office, such as family photos and mementos
✓ decorations that show people more than things
✓ an emphasis on people in their communications
✓ a preference to meet in a less formal setting, away from the office
✓ a focus on benefits for people
✓ a tendency to be more open to listening and compromise

To influence feeling people, you should

✓ show the benefits of your product/service to the human side of the organization
✓ avoid a strong emphasis on monetary benefits

✓ behave in an open, warm, and friendly way
✓ take an interest in the buyer on a personal level

167 Thinking people make decisions based on logic. They prefer

✓ appearing impersonal
✓ focusing on the bottom line
✓ being brief and businesslike
✓ analyzing the smallest details

You can easily spot a thinker, because they tend to

✓ be neatly and conservatively dressed
✓ have more electronic gadgets than average
✓ ask tough questions
✓ appear blunt and to the point

To influence thinkers, you need to

✓ get to the point quickly
✓ prove your case with figures, charts, and facts
✓ prove your case based on merit
✓ dress conservatively

168 Intuitive people are forward-looking and tend to be creative in their problem solving. They are distinguished by

✓ creativity
✓ a keen intellect
✓ interest in "the big picture"

You can spot an intuitive person by noticing

✓ their questions, which focus on issues rather than details
✓ reference or philosophy books on their shelves
✓ abstract art and charts on the wall

To influence intuitive people, you need to

✓ describe benefits in relation to the long-term future
✓ describe benefits in general terms
✓ show her how your product/service fits into the overall strategy of the client organization

✓ allow time for them to imagine benefits

169 Sensing people tend to operate in the world by making effective use of their five senses: taste, touch, smell, sight, and hearing. They tend to be:

✓ detail-oriented
✓ decisive
✓ pragmatic
✓ impatient

You can spot a sensing person because they:

✓ focus on what's in front of them instead of on the future
✓ think aloud (talk before thinking)
✓ usually has a messy office
✓ is surrounded by action pictures on the wall
✓ dresses more casually, without a jacket or tie

To influence sensing people, you need to:

✓ focus on getting things done, suggesting action steps
✓ be brief and to the point
✓ show examples, allowing them to see, touch, and smell (if appropriate) what you are offering
✓ present only viable options to expedite decision making

Estée Lauder put it well when she said, "If you don't sell, it's not the product that's wrong, it's you!"

How to...
Be savvy

Leaders need to be savvy. Savvy people get things done. They understand, are well informed, and are perceptive about their surroundings. They are able to navigate the political morass that surrounds them. They understand the organization's culture and are able to get things done in spite of the boundaries that are sometimes created. They are able to overcome resistance and work cooperatively even with difficult people. They understand risks and how far they can push the boundaries without becoming exposed.

With this in mind, here are some strategies that will make you more savvy:

170 Study the organization's culture. Take your time before taking risks. Find out who has succeeded and why they have done so. Find out as well who has failed and what led to their downfall.

171 Learn about the reward system. What actions get you formal rewards and informal recognition? And find out what types of actions can lead to censure or worse.

172 Research the power networks. Who are the people who wield power? Find out how they do so and why. Before you discuss personalities in anything but a glowing fashion, know about the people connected to those you wish to share confidential information with.

173 Develop a positive disposition. Smile often. Become the resident optimist. Look for solutions and present them with enthusiasm when others are focused on obstacles, roadblocks, and problems.

174 Become to "go-to" person. Be a resource for others. Offer help, especially advice, whenever asked.

175 Offer to give leadership to difficult situations, especially high-profile problems. Work your tail off to turn a mess into an opportunity, especially when others are throwing their hands up in the air.

176 Get involved in cross-cultural initiatives within and beyond your work area. These are opportunities to demonstrate empathy, understanding, and appreciation of other cultures – skills that are much in demand as the working world shrinks.

177 Understand power. Learn to maximize your power in positive ways. Influence people around you by

✓ expressing your opinions confidently – leaning forward, maintaining eye contact and speaking with a firm, but pleasant tone
✓ being factual wherever possible rather than offering opinions that can easily be shot down
✓ citing examples where you or others have had success in similar circumstances
✓ never threatening to do something unless you are willing to carry through on it

178 Make a statement whenever you enter a room. Walk tall. Smile. Shake as many hands as you can. Think of yourself as the president even if you're not. Imagine that the people gathered are here for a special occasion – to celebrate your birthday or promotion. Introduce people to each other as if they were your long-time friends.

179 Participate in high-profile projects with a high probability of success. Avoid those that are likely to stall or are staffed by people who resemble pit bulls.

180 Behave like a service provider rather than a service user. View people in positions of power as clients. Don't meet their expectations, exceed them.

181 Find out things of personal interest to the power figures. Engage them in casual conversations while standing in the line at the cafeteria. Pay them compliments (but don't be patronizing).

How to...
Influence people

*A spoonful of honey will catch more flies
than a gallon of vinegar.*

– BENJAMIN FRANKLIN

No matter what their rank, *people in your workplace are
dependent on everyone else. We influence our peers, bosses, and
subordinates at work daily, and they influence us. The trick is
to influence them positively – to get buy-in to your ideas and
projects.*

182 Develop a cooperative and team-oriented outlook. Think
of your colleagues as resources and friends rather than
competitors for brownie points or promotions.

183 Don't pull rank. Don't leave your boss out of the loop. It may
work once but will lead to distrust. You won't be privy to
confidential information in future, nor will you be consulted
regarding how to solve problems. And you certainly won't be
given credit to those in senior positions when you otherwise
may have deserved it.

184 Treat people with respect. Recognize the person for what
they bring to the organization. You don't have to like everything about them or the way they do things, but life is a lot
easier when you make people feel valued.

185 Find out what motivates the people you need to work with. Treat each one as special and always let them know, whenever they exceed your expectations, that you value their contribution. Acknowledge their efforts in small but meaningful ways so they know they're on the right track and their efforts are appreciated.

186 Deal with differences directly whether they're peers or subordinates. Don't appeal to those above you to exert influence, because that will keep you from developing on your own. And don't bad-mouth them behind their backs; you can never be sure that word won't get back to them. And if it does, work life will become more hellish than it may be at present.

187 Understand your workplace barter. Workplaces run on a formal or informal exchange of favors and unique skills. You have some, your boss has some, your subordinates have some, and they are all different. Be sure to offer favors so you can collect at some stage too. Find out what each person's forte is, and how you can do them a favor to make sure you have access to that talent in the future.

188 Relationships are a two-way street. Be kind, thoughtful, and empathetic with others and they will be the same with you. Be impatient, impolite, and rude with them and...Well, you get the picture.

How to...
Create win-win outcomes when conflict looms

The measure of a man is what he does with power.

– PITTACUS OF MYTILENE

Negotiating is the ability to influence people. It is the art of letting someone else have your way. Most people have no idea how easy it is to influence others. People have a lot more power to influence than they believe. There are many ways you can use power to help you achieve your objective. Study and use these approaches to maximize your influence:

189 Consider your approach when differences loom. Are you naturally combative? Are you focused on persuasion or problem solving? Are the first words that come out of your mouth, "Yeah, but...?"

Listen to Understand

190 Avoid starting each sentence with "but." If your inclination is to be argumentative, learn to listen deeply. Understand why people have a different approach than yours. Is there some legitimacy to their issues? Are they debating out of a sense of frustration because they never get their way with you? Or do they have some legitimate issues that should be acknowledged?

191 Look for points of commonality so you and they can get onto the same side of the issue. Whenever there are points of agreement, point them out by summarizing, "So, what I'm hearing is we both agree that..."

Do Your Homework

192 Before any significant negotiation, understand where your opponent is coming from, what they have to offer and where they may be challenged. Consider which issues may become "show stoppers" and the issues on which they are likely to offer a compromise.

Be flexible and creative.

193 Issues are rarely black or white. Consider alternatives where both parties can benefit or at the least not lose face. Give options instead of treats or ultimatums.

Set the Tone

194 Create an atmosphere of congeniality. Use humor to tone down the temperature when tension is preventing each side from seeing possible wins.

195 Recognize good points and show agreement when good arguments are made. This will reduce tension and emotion allowing others to open their minds to your good points.

196 Learn to compromise or acquiesce, especially on minor points, and you will find your "opponent" will do so more readily too.

Ask for the Order!

197 There comes a time when you need to bring closure. Don't be afraid to suggest that you have an agreement and confirm that this is so. If not, ask what else needs to be done to bring about closure.

198 Use your power positively. We all have much more power than we think. Spend the time to think about how you can maximize your power and be very convincing, especially in dealing with critical issues. Power strategies include:

✓ *Precedent.* Show examples where your idea has worked before. The best precedents come from your own work area or organization. If you can't find examples from close to home, look within your industry. When presenting ideas using precedent, say "I know it will work because it has done so before. Here's an example."

✓ *Legitimacy.* Make your idea look legitimate by using documentation. Written reports will enhance a verbal presentation. Information from trade journals citing examples of success or quoting acknowledged experts will all improve your case. When you introduce legitimacy, you might say, "Here is an example of what I am talking about" or "Here is additional evidence regarding what I am saying."

✓ *Persistence.* If water drops on a rock, it will eventually make a hole in it. Similarly, you will wear down your opposition if you are tenacious. You will demonstrate persistence by refusing to take no for an answer. Keep wearing your opponent down with comments like, "Yes, but..." or "When else could we meet?" or "Let's keep trying till we do find a way."

✓ *Competition.* Let people know you have choices. They will feel less secure knowing your needs can be satisfied elsewhere. So you can say, "If you can't, then I will ask X" or "I can get more from Y."

✓ *Knowledge.* Let people know about your expertise. Show them your qualifications (legitimacy). The more impressed they are with your credentials, the easier it will be to influence them. Also, demonstrate your knowledge with facts and examples of where you have been successful before (precedent).

✓ *Rationality.* Give people the data to back up your opinions. Presenting the data in writing (legitimacy) will further increase your power.

✓ *Rank.* You can use rank positively or negatively. If people think you will make a decision regardless of their opinion because your rank allows you to, they will find ways to subvert the implementation. So if you use rank, do so only as a last resort, reminding people only momentarily of your position. You can also increase your power by linking with people who have a higher rank. For example, say, "The president told me that..."

IV

How to...
INSPIRE AND MOTIVATE STAFF

Lessons 199–385

How to...
Be a great coach

The final test of a leader is that he leaves behind
in other men the conviction and the will to carry on.

– WALTER LIPPMANN

Coaching is a process that will let your employees know that what they do and who they are matters to you.

Good coaches train their people to do the job right every time. Most coaching focuses on the technical areas of a job, but can also be used to improve people's team and interpersonal skills.

199 Create the environment in which people will be receptive to coaching and excelling in their tasks. Do this by

   ✓ getting to know your people on a personal level
   ✓ finding out what people do well in their personal lives and finding ways to use those skills in the workplace
   ✓ spending time with people, especially when they have ideas to share or concerns to voice. This will demonstrate your interest and respect for them.

200 Meet daily with people – either collectively or one on one – to make sure they know what is expected of them. Involve them if there are any unexpected challenges that require some creative problem solving.

201 Take the time to meet each month for a longer period to demonstrate that you care about them and their task. Most organizations are frustrating places to work in. So listening empathetically to your employee's issues and helping them to overcome challenges will cement your bond with each member of your team

202 Coach each person according to their ability and willingness to demonstrate responsibility. You will need to give explicit instructions to those who are untrained or unwilling. Those who are competent and mature need fewer instructions and can be given broader discretion. The superstars can be left to do what they know is right because they will overcome challenges when and where they occur or check in with you if necessary.

203 Measure each person's performance. Allow them to have input into the best indicator(s). Track their performance to see whether they're improving or need more coaching.

204 Encourage people to be aware of their performance and take ownership of improvement.

205 Never let good work go unnoticed. Recognize improved performance. Small celebrations that combine simplicity and sincerity are best.

206 If performance declines, do not give the correct action before trying to get the employee to solve the problem. This is how you teach them to think for themselves and develop self-esteem. You should give an answer only if the employee cannot solve the problem, it needs to be done urgently, or if a health and safety issue is involved.

207 Establish best practices for key tasks. Document them and train each associate to follow the one best method. Always be open to change the documentation as new and improved methods are established.

208 Use these methods to help your associates become stars:

✓ *Demonstrating.* Show your associates how the task can best be done.

✓ *Documenting.* Record the best and correct way to do the task and encourage your associates to follow your instructions on their own.

✓ *Facilitating.* Help your associates find solutions by asking open-ended questions and prompting step-by-step self-discovery.

✓ *Training.* Increase your associates' skills with on-the-job training. Start by explaining what you want them to do, then show them how to do it, let them try while you observe, and give them feedback on their performance.

✓ *Confronting.* Let your associates know when their performance fails to meet agreed-upon standards.

✓ *Redirecting.* If associates make mistakes, show them again. Focus on the mistake, not the person, or you will undermine their confidence. Get them to confirm their understanding. Then, have them demonstrate their understanding by showing you how to do the task.

209 If the task is large or appears difficult, break it into pieces. Learning one step at a time will build the trainee's self-confidence.

210 If associates do not improve after a number of trials, determine whether the cause is attitudinal or a lack of aptitude. If it is the latter, move the associate to jobs that suit their skill sets better. If it is attitudinal, determine the cause and solution. If this still does not work – and only a small minority will not respond – go through the disciplinary procedure and terminate the individual.

211 Give people regular feedback. Wherever possible, let associates know when they have done well and also when they have failed to meet your expectations.

212 As people's skills improve, encourage them to discover new and better ways of doing things. Praise them for their new ideas. Incorporate their ideas into daily improved procedures.

213 Allow people to improvise. Even if the new method does not fit your perception of the best solution, encourage a spirit of enterprise.

How to...
Develop a high-performance team culture

A mediocre idea that generates enthusiasm
will go further than a great idea that inspires no one.

– MARY KAY ASH

*M**aintaining performance at a high level** for the benefit of your customers is essential. You can sustain and improve performance if you*

214 Have a focus. Create a Mission Statement collectively so everyone on the team has a sense of purpose.

215 Measure team performance to ensure that your activities match your intentions. Post your key performance indicators where everyone can see them. Show the team its results graphically so they can see whether they're doing better or worse in terms of:

✓ quality
✓ timeliness
✓ cost effectiveness
✓ staff morale

216 Display these measures prominently so employees can track the impact of their efforts immediately.

217 Set team, rather than individual, goals using key performance indicators (KPIs).

218 Break your team into mini-teams that will collect the data for one or a cluster of KPIs. Have them also take responsibility for creating plans to achieve their stretch goals. This will build trust, ensure enthusiasm, and develop a sense of ownership for implementing the plans.

219 Review performance regularly to see whether the implemented ideas have brought about the anticipated improvements. Were there any significant changes in performance?

220 Sustain the improvements. Note what actions were taken to bring about the improvements. Make sure these are repeated and shared with other people in the organization who might also benefit.

221 Celebrate significant improvements. Recognition can be as simple as a "thank you" at a spontaneous meeting on the shop floor or a lunch off-site. Some teams develop their own ceremonies and symbols like ringing a bell when new records have been established. Encourage unique ways of celebrating, even though they may be out of character with the corporate culture.

222 If performance declines, don't look for victims. Involve the team in problem solving. Find out why performance has dropped and ask for ideas on how to improve.

223 Develop action plans for improvement. Involve the team in this process. Develop a list of actions with specific dates for implementation. Ask team members to take responsibility

224 Celebrate team successes. Make this a part of your regular meetings. Celebrations should be spontaneous and informal. There are dozens of ways to celebrate, such as ordering in treats, having your boss come by to congratulate the team, or sending team members an e-mail message of congratulations and copying your boss.

225 Promote team problem solving. Keep a flip chart handy so any time there is a problem that requires team input, you can collect ideas on the causes and the solutions. Write them down, prioritize each list, and then create an action plan on the most popular solution.

226 Strike a balance between sharing challenges with your employees that they need to know about and burdening them with problems they can't do much about.

227 Be accessible for consultation with your employees if problems arise, but don't micromanage. Encourage them to consult each other, solving problems collaboratively.

228 Establish a guideline that whenever employees bring you a problem, they are expected to also bring you a possible solution. Encourage them to discuss their ideas among themselves so final suggestions have the support of the team.

229 Balance peak work periods with some less stressful activities. Take time to do fun activities together, such as bowling, dining out, or sharing ethnic foods during lunch.

230 Recognize when your people are putting in extra effort. Acknowledge and thank them in a way that seems appropriate. Many people appreciate handwritten notes from the boss.

231 When it's practical and appropriate, give tangible rewards. But be careful not to create an environment of entitlement.

232 Celebrate the completion of a demanding project. Acknowledge special efforts or contributions made by individuals, but make sure that the team is also recognized.

233 Help your team learn from unexpected challenges. Review what went well and what mistakes were made that could be handled differently next time around.

234 Find out what gets in the way of the team doing their best. If red tape, bureaucracy, or politics interfere with their productivity, do what you can to buffer or eliminate those barriers.

235 Delegate, but don't abdicate. Giving the team challenging problems to solve will promote collaboration, learning, and growth. Don't set them up for failure, however; ensure that they have the knowledge, skills, and resources they need to succeed.

236 Hold yourself to the same standards you expect of others. Few people are inspired by those who adhere to a double standard.

237 Don't ask your people to do anything you wouldn't do yourself. In fact, from time to time, show your interest in their work by working alongside them to get an understanding of the challenges they face so you can respond better when they have difficulties.

238 Don't ask associates to do anything illegal or unethical. Doing so establishes an environment that will deteriorate and lead to your demise.

239 Set standards that require people to stretch but that aren't impossible to achieve.

240 Give feedback in a fair, transparent manner. When you have concerns about an employee's performance, communicate those concerns directly with that team member. Don't make negative comments about a team member to other people on the team.

How to...
Encourage collaboration in your team

I'm just a plow hand from Arkansas, but I have learned how to hold a team together ... how to lift some men up, how to calm down others, until they've got one heartbeat together.

– BEAR BRYANT

Nothing influences behavior more than your performance as a leader. You are the role model and your actions, not the slogans on the wall, will influence how others behave. For your organization to succeed, cultivate a collaborative environment. Encourage working together, both within and between teams, for a common purpose. Here are some strategies to make this happen:

241 Cultivate a team environment. Use the word "team" instead of "department" or "unit" when communicating with your associates.

242 Meet often – formally and informally – to discuss team initiatives, plans, activities, and performance.

243 Encourage openness. Don't allow associates to talk behind each other's backs. Teach them to discuss differences openly and respectfully.

244 Have fun together. Look for opportunities to laugh together. You can deal with issues in an open and relaxed manner and still be serious about your work.

245 Greet employees by name when you make first contact each day. If you have a large number of employees, don't be afraid to ask them to remind you of their name, this shows that you really want to remember them.

246 Engage in small talk with your employees when the opportunity presents itself. Get to know more about their interests and goals and something of their personal life, if they are willing to share. Encourage them to share those parts of their lives outside of work with each other too.

247 Be a positive, encouraging force. When an individual or the team as a whole seems tired or discouraged, acknowledge their feelings and show appreciation for their efforts. Small gestures like a note of appreciation or even showing up with coffee and doughnuts at just the right moment can boost morale.

248 Be willing to roll up your sleeves and work as hard as you expect your team members to work. Your main role may be to coach from the sidelines, but there may also be occasions when you have to get involved in the game yourself. Don't be afraid to get your hands dirty. You don't have to be down in the trenches every minute, but situations that call for extra manpower or superhuman effort are opportunities for you to inspire your people by working alongside them. The times when bosses stay until midnight with their employees to finish a project or solve a problem become the stuff of corporate legend.

249 Give regular feedback to members on team performance. Your feedback will build involvement, commitment, and a sense of pride as results improve. It will also build trust with associates as they realize that you will always address issues of concern with them personally and not behind their backs.

250 Celebrate improvements to promote a sense of pride and team cohesiveness. Keep these occasions brief and informal. Always show recognition in a way that's appropriate for the person and the occasion. Simple, spontaneous recognition at the moment of achievement, or very soon thereafter, is best.

251 Recruit new members whose personalities, work ethic, and values will be compatible with those of the group. In fact, involve the group in finding and selecting new members so they have an additional commitment to making the induction process successful.

252 Know when to step in and when to stay out of team conflicts. A certain amount of disagreement is not only normal but essential for any team challenging itself to reach new and higher levels. But if a conflict between two or more associates is polarizing the group and creating unnecessary tension, it may be time for you to step in. Consider bringing in a skilled mediator if you feel you don't have the skills to mediate effectively.

253 Plan occasional team events that let people get together without the pressures of work. These may be a monthly lunch to celebrate team members' birthdays or a semi-annual off-site planning day that includes time to socialize. Be creative if you have budget constraints. Make sure these are events that everyone can participate in.

254 Minimize the impact of a destructive team member. If you inherit a problematic employee or hire someone who turns out to have negative effects on the team's morale, find out what is interfering with that person's ability to be a positive, productive worker.

    ✓ If the personality problem is solvable, such as transferring the associate to another area, do what you can to resolve the situation.

✓ If the person must stay, clarify your expectations for improvement, and, if necessary, what the consequences might be if no improvement is forthcoming.

✓ If you are simply stuck with a negative employee you can't terminate, do what you can to minimize this person's effect on others (for example, you could assign tasks they can do on their own).

255 Be loyal to your team. Remember that loyalty is a two-way street. Demonstrate your loyalty when it counts, such as

✓ being the voice of your team at the management table. If you don't advocate for their needs and give voice to their opinions, no one else will. However, ensure that your employees know it is your role to balance their needs with the needs of the organization.

✓ sharing the credit with your team for its achievements and ensuring that those above you know about its successes

256 Avoid pointing a finger when something goes wrong. If one or more team members have let the team down, address the situation with those people but don't broadcast it at meetings or chastise the whole team for the actions of one or two.

257 Encourage the development of a team subculture. This can include the team creating its own name and having unique ways of celebrating successes. The group will develop its own ceremonies and symbols to promote its sense of being unique.

258 Expect a lot. Challenge people at all times. Let them know the extent of your confidence in them.

259 Encourage job rotation, if your technology allows it. Benefits include:

✓ less monotony
✓ learning new skills
✓ personal growth
✓ empathy for one another's problems
✓ shared ownership of performance
✓ improved productivity
✓ less downtime

260 Encourage people to get to know one another on a personal level without unduly invading anyone's privacy.

261 Recruit people with well-developed interpersonal skills and a positive attitude. Knowing how to listen, give feedback, and manage conflict are critical skills for effective team members.

262 Involve the team in the decision to recruit new members. This will increase the likelihood of achieving a good "fit" as well as ensuring that the new recruit will integrate more quickly and successfully into the team.

263 Establish ground rules that govern team behavior. These may include such simple items as agreeing to

✓ pitch in and help each other
✓ share the workload
✓ always be open and honest with each other
✓ be tolerant of and respectful of differences in personality
✓ meet deadlines the team has committed to

264 Allow members to monitor and deal with transgressors.

265 Reward behavior that goes above and beyond your values and ground rules.

266 Care about your people. You don't need to be their best friend or their personal counselor (nor should you be). However, getting to know them beyond saying "good morning" will allow you to find out what motivates and inspires them to give their all.

How to...
Use measurement to motivate people and teams

> *The only man who behaved sensibly was my tailor;*
> *he took my measurement anew every time he saw me,*
> *while all the rest went on with their old*
> *measurements and expected them to fit me.*
>
> *– GEORGE BERNARD SHAW*

If you don't measure something, you won't be able to manage it. The most effective way to measure your team's performance is to involve your associates and customers in the process. Creating a balanced approach in choosing key performance indicators will enhance the impact of your measurement system. Balance can be achieved in two ways:

- *choosing indicators that measure the past as well as the future*

- *picking indicators that allow you to track the team's ability to meet the needs of its various stakeholders*

Here is a simple but powerful way to measure your team's performance.

Step 1: Determine your readiness

267 Evaluate your chances of a radical change in the way you measure your team's performance. Your readiness will be high if you:

✓ tend to have a participative style of management
✓ share information readily with associates
✓ have a high state of morale
✓ take a constructive approach to dealing with problems
✓ have good, accurate, and reliable measurement systems in place
✓ regularly and spontaneously celebrate achievements and innovative ideas and actions

Step 2: Inform your associates of the changes you would like to see

268 Have a meeting to share your vision of how the team could benefit from a more effective approach to measurement. Get their feedback on the process you are proposing, one that will

✓ require active involvement and support of the people whose performance it is measuring
✓ measure the performance as it relates to all stakeholders
✓ be the focus of future team meetings
✓ require team members to collect data and report on their performance each month
✓ encourage team problem solving and goal setting
✓ enable associates to constantly challenge the way business is being conducted
✓ transfer ownership for performance from the team's manager to the team plus its manager

Step 3: Understand and define your work system

269 Research is the first step. Work with your associates to answer the following questions:

✓ Who are our customers, both internal and external?
✓ What do they expect from us?

- ✓ How are these expectations being acknowledged and measured?
- ✓ How should they be measured?
- ✓ What products or services are we currently supplying?
- ✓ What resources are we using to meet our customers' needs? A description of the primary resources (people, materials, methods, equipment, and capital) should be documented.

Step 4: Define what you would like to do and document your mission

270 Your team should document its mission. A simple formula for writing up a mission is to answer these six questions:

- ✓ Who are we?
- ✓ What do we do?
- ✓ How do we provide the product or service?
- ✓ Whom do we serve?
- ✓ Where are our customers?
- ✓ Why do we exist?

Once these questions are answered, wordsmith them until they form a clear, crisp sentence. Modify the wording until the message is as clear and simple as possible.

Step 4: Identify Key Performance Indicators

271 Your mission statement will list your stakeholders. The next task is to identify indicators for tracking success in meeting the needs and expectations of your mission. If you have done your research (Step 1) thoroughly, it should be relatively easy to identify indicators in a variety of categories, such as:

- ✓ external and internal client/customer requirements such as quality, timeliness, and value
- ✓ management requirements for income enhancement, cost containment, productivity improvement, and innovation

✓ employees' need for work satisfaction, health and safety, and training and development

272 Your associates should reach consensus on each indicator. Their input and agreement will build commitment that focuses on these key issues. Where possible, pick indicators that:

✓ are easy to collect
✓ are already being collected
✓ are accurate
✓ you have control over

Step 5: Determine existing performance levels for each indicator

273 Average the performance of the previous three months or another period to get a sense of what performance will look like if no changes are made.

✓ As you gather data, you will see how suitable your index is. If, for example, it becomes extremely costly to collect data for an indicator, then the value of the indicator should be questioned.

Step 6: Establish objectives for each indicator

274 Set goals. The goals should be SMART:

- **S** pecific
- **M** easurable
- **A** greed-upon
- **R** ealistic
- **T** ime-based.

✓ Setting objectives will be difficult the first time around. Some team members will be optimistic and set unreasonably challenging goals. Other might be cautious and set very modest goals, hoping to ensure that they're achieved without too much difficulty. A rational approach would be to benchmark the team's scores against past performance, other teams doing similar work, or teams in other organizations that do similar tasks. The further afield one looks for information, the more the team will be exposed to best practices that may help them achieve extraordinary results.

Step 7: Establish mini-objectives

275 Establish a set of mini-objectives for each month or quarter that will lead you toward the ultimate annual objective.

Step 8: Post your measures

276 Set up a line or bar graph for each indicator showing existing performance and comparisons with past performance and objectives.

Step 9: Organize and plan improvement strategies

277 Create mini-teams for each key performance indicator. The leader of the team is generally known as the focal. The focal and team members will meet regularly to

- ✓ establish that their index is accurate and easy to collect
- ✓ confirm whether the established current performance levels on which objectives have been set are reasonable
- ✓ collect data each month to track changes in performance
- ✓ report the reasons for changes, whether good or bad, at team meetings
- ✓ make suggestions for changes based on their own ideas, research, and input from members outside of their mini-team
- ✓ help implement ongoing changes and improvements

How to...
Motivate your associates

*He who loses money, loses much; he who loses a friend,
loses much more; he who loses faith, loses all.*

*A**s a leader,** your treatment of others will have a major impact
on their enthusiasm and commitment. Here are some things you
can do to bring out the best in people.*

278 Have high expectations. See them all as "A" grade employees.
The more you expect from people, the more

   ✓ you will change your behavior to become enthusiastic
   ✓ your challenges will increase
   ✓ your energy and enthusiasm will rise
   ✓ you will demonstrate trust
   ✓ you will delegate and empower
   ✓ your employees will respond

279 Listen. Keep your ear to the ground. Identify issues that
might cause poor morale and take swift action to deal deci-
sively with problems. Set time aside for focus groups to allow
people to identify concerns you can address on their behalf.

280 Recognize superior effort and achievement. Show your
appreciation in a timely fashion and in a personal way. Be

specific about the achievement. You can show your pleasure in dozens of ways, including:

✓ private verbal appreciation
✓ public recognition
✓ a handwritten note
✓ an e-mail with a copy to someone really important
✓ a note in the person's file

281 Pay people well. If possible, pay at the highest percentile of your industry. People are almost always your most under-utilized resource; you can demonstrate your faith in them through your compensation system. People who feel under-paid never give one hundred percent. In fact, they give as little as possible. Keeping salaries low seldom ends up in lower costs.

282 Pay attention to your language and the way you treat people. You are the role model; others will evaluate your behavior.

283 Show an interest in your associates. Actions speak louder than words. Set time aside each month to demonstrate you care for them as whole people by meeting for up to two hours one-on-one with each of them. At these meetings

✓ review their goals and objectives
✓ see how they're progressing
✓ identify learning and training opportunities
✓ identify special skills they could impart to others
✓ get a sense of their level of motivation and problem-solve with them the obstacles that may be hindering them
✓ plan new challenges for the month ahead
✓ follow up on items of personal interest that the two of you share

284 Refer to employees as "our people" or "associates." Do not use demeaning and impersonal descriptions such as "full-time equivalents," "billing units," or other demeaning descriptions.

285 Treat your people with respect. This means listening to them, being willing to try their ideas, and avoiding punishment when genuinely unfortunate mistakes are made.

286 Treat mistakes as a natural part of growing and learning. Allow associates to self-correct and to identify better ways of dealing with the situation if it occurs again.

287 Don't tell associates what to do unless time is short, you are the expert, or health and safety codes are in jeopardy. Rather, ask them to do things for you. When doing so, make sure that your tone and body language show enthusiasm and confidence.

288 Measure associates' performance (outcomes) so you don't have to monitor them all the time.

289 Sell associates on new ideas. Don't simply tell them to implement your ideas because you are in a position of power, especially if the idea is likely to be unpopular.

290 View your associates as contributors, not costs. Treat them in a way that makes them feel important, not expendable.

291 Award spontaneous bonuses for exceptional achievement. Don't publicize the process in case you create expectations. Pay bonuses in various amounts at different times so they are a surprise and seen as genuine appreciation for a job well done.

292 Set objectives with employees. Everyone needs to know what you expect of them. Document those goals and monitor progress toward them.

293 Remember your employees' significant others and partners. Often your people will be called on to put in extra effort that may require them to work longer hours or over a weekend.

Send the significant other some acknowledgment in return for their support such as a card, flowers, or a voucher for a meal for two. If you're on the road and have invited someone to dinner, offer to host their partner too.

294 Make work a joy to the full extent possible. Have fun. Look for opportunities to bring people together to laugh. Business is serious, but people will be more motivated if they have reason to smile.

295 Use the HR department as a resource, when needed. Redefine the role of the HR department, if necessary. But remember that the responsibility for staff morale remains the challenge of line managers. The HR department is there to mentor you and give you the knowledge and tools to bring out the best in your associates.

296 If you have the power, make the head of HR an executive position that reports directly to the president, not to the VP of finance.

How to...
Delegate

The highest manifestation of life is this: that a being governs its own actions. A thing that is always subject to the direction of another is somewhat of a dead thing.

– St. Thomas Aquinas

As a leader, you will be judged not only by what happens when you are present, but even more so by what happens when you are absent.

Good managers never put off till tomorrow what they can delegate today. A major cause of stress and poor time management is the unwillingness, or inability, to delegate responsibility to employees. Delegating responsibility to others allows you to concentrate on management and leadership duties such as planning, problem solving, and other proactive matters. Failure to delegate forces you to spend too much time on the trivial issues your associates should be taking care of. Here's how to take the monkey off your back:

297 Prepare for a new approach with some serious soul searching. Accept that you cannot do everything, be everywhere, and make all of the decisions. Believe that your people are capable of doing more of your mundane work without much difficulty. Ask yourself

   ✓ Why has delegation been difficult in the past?
   ✓ Do I enjoy doing the work I am accustomed to handling?

✓ Do I have little faith in my associates?

✓ Are my associates inadequately trained?

✓ Have I failed to establish standards of performance?

✓ Are procedures inadequately documented or not documented at all?

✓ Does my boss expect me to be overly involved in day-to-day activities?

Correct any problems uncovered before moving forward.

298 Write down all of your activities for one week. Categorize them as A activities (critical, for the benefit of your client/customer or boss), B activities (not critically impacting your reputation), C activities (fun, but unnecessary). Usually, most of the A activities can be delegated because they include:

✓ routine work

✓ data collection

✓ attending meetings that are unrelated to benefiting any internal or external clients

299 Pay greater attention to the B tasks that are more enriching and require enhanced brainpower. These activities will use your conceptual and communication abilities, including

✓ strategic planning

✓ coaching

✓ goal setting

✓ communicating new information

✓ problem solving

✓ liaising with customers

✓ carrying messages between those above and below you

300 Meet with your associates and let them know about your change of heart, findings, and plans so they understand and buy into to your new approach and don't see it as a chance for you to dump additional work onto them. Stress the benefits for everyone – the department, yourself, and the employees.

301 Identify associates who could take some of the load off your shoulders. These employees

✓ demonstrate an interest in their work
✓ have or will make the time to take on more responsibility
✓ have the skills or are able to learn the additional task/duty

302 If people have the time and inclination but not the skills, train them.

303 Set up a meeting with the appropriate associate(s). At the meeting

✓ Explain the purpose of your discussion.

✓ Describe the task you want done.

✓ Explain why they were chosen. Put a positive spin on the reason so they feel special and responsible.

✓ Discuss benefits they might enjoy as a result of taking on the new job. These may include increased responsibility, learning opportunities, added exposure in the organization, or promotion opportunities.

✓ Be specific about the objective so they know exactly what is expected and when and how the task needs to be done.

✓ Stress how important it is for the task to be done in a timely and accurate manner.

✓ Get agreement on the objective.

✓ If the task is large, establish mini-goals with corresponding time lines.

✓ Make sure the person accepts the task and its scope. A handshake is an acceptable way of acknowledging acceptance.

✓ If the task is complex, give directions in writing to ensure that there is no ambiguity – you don't want the associate to have to constantly rely on their memory of your expectations.

✓ Assign responsibility and authority. Stress your confidence in your associate's ability to do the job.

✓ Ask if the associate foresees any problems in carrying out the task. Help to resolve any problems. Stress that your door is always open should they run into problems.

304 Follow up with the associate. Monitor their progress as needed to ensure directions are clearly understood and the job is being done as expected.

305 Monitor performance closely at first and then less frequently. If associates are performing well, let them know. If not, give them appropriate feedback, focusing on the behavior, not the person.

306 Show confidence in your associates by being open to their suggestions if they find a new way to do the task that is as good or better.

307 Ensure that people who work with you and your associate know you have delegated the task and have given the associate the authority to do the job.

How to...
Engage and empower your staff

> *The rung of a ladder was never meant to rest upon,*
> *but only to hold a person's foot long enough*
> *to enable him to put the other somewhat higher.*
>
> *– ALDOUS HUXLEY*

Little has changed over the last couple of decades. The biggest issue demotivating employees is their feeling that they lack control – that their ideas are unimportant and they are not permitted to make changes, even small ones, without asking for permission. This lack of power makes employees feel helpless, useless, and undervalued. The longer it continues, the more self-fulfilling it becomes. People will behave the way they are treated.

Your employees should always be regarded as an asset to protect and develop. You will find you get the best results as a manager when you treat people as partners, increasing their level of authority as their skills and responsibilities increase. Here's what you can do:

308 Take stock of your attitude toward others. In general, do you have faith in others and look forward to listening to them and their ideas? Or are you so arrogant you feel that you have little to learn from those lower on the totem pole?

309 Realize that you are not an oracle. You are not knowledge-able about everything; there is always an opportunity to learn from others.

310 Assess each individual's willingness to be empowered. Each one has a different level of need. The best employees see additional power as a vote of confidence in their ability. This motivates them to live up to your vision of them.

311 Avoid failure by assessing the person's ability to exercise the new power. Make sure they are properly trained beforehand.

312 Make sure people know the limits of their authority. Consider increasing their power when they show confidence and ability to excel within those limits.

313 Allow your associates some latitude in finding their own path to achieving the objective(s).

314 If something goes wrong, don't fix the mistake (unless it is a major issue, involves health and safety, or is an emergency of some other type) without giving the associate a chance to do it themselves. They will learn to be responsible for their own decisions only if they have an opportunity to learn from their own errors.

315 Monitor your management systems (decision making, infor-mation flow, selection, authority, accountability) frequently to make sure these systems encourage staff performance rather than present obstacles to it.

316 Increase the skills and confidence of your work group by making training an ongoing activity. Provide many ways of training, including classroom instruction, peer training on the job, self-directed reading of manuals, and videos and workshops, to name a few.

317 If people are reluctant to assume new responsibilities, be patient. Try to make it clear to them that they, as well as you and the organization, will benefit from their increased effort and skills.

318 Be consistently supportive of your associates. Winning their trust will make them more willing to take on new challenges.

How to...
Shine by accepting increased responsibility

There are two ways of exerting one's strength:
One is pushing down, the other is pulling up.

– *Booker T. Washington*

Most employees *have found the concept of empowerment hollow and without meaning. While the idea raises the expectations of people to the possibilities of being treated like responsible adults, the reality is that most front-line people can't buy a three-hole punch without approval. If your organization is proclaiming the new religion of empowerment, here's how you can benefit:*

319 Meet with your boss. Ask:

✓ how the new management philosophy will impact you as a manager and how much authority and responsibility you are expected to give to your direct reports. Press for specifics. If nothing is forthcoming, give your own examples, such as, "Can I allow my employees to settle clients' claims for up to one hundred dollars without my approval?" If the reaction is positive, you're likely to see some meaningful change. If not, and you get a "Yes, but ..." response, lower your expectations and expect little change.

✓ to identify specific barriers that prevent more decisions

being made by members of your team. If lack of training is an issue, offer to create and implement a training plan that will give staff the confidence and competence to make larger decisions.

✓ what the consequences might be for mistakes given that your staff will be making increasingly bigger decisions.

320 If you are a team-based organization, there will be an expectation that you and your team will become increasingly self-managed. This presents exciting possibilities. You should encourage your team to meet to identify

✓ existing boundaries and parameters
✓ new potential boundaries
✓ increased responsibilities for such things as
  • who will run team meetings,
  • how you will decide on allocating work,
  • who will schedule holidays and how
  • how will you deal with conflict,
  • who will be responsible for hiring decisions
  • how will decisions be made.

321 If you are in a unionized organization and are part of the bargaining unit, you may be discouraged from doing things that are deemed to be managerial in nature. If you are in doubt, discuss the issue with your boss and your shop steward.

322 Some increased responsibilities may change the nature of your job. Your job classification could be impacted too, enabling you to earn more. If this is the case, consult your boss and people from human resources for advice.

How to...
Challenge your staff with stretch goals and objectives

You can't hit a target you cannot see,
and you cannot see a target you do not have.

– ZIG ZIGLAR

Without **direction**, *employees are doomed to operate aimlessly, adding little value to the organization and its stake-holders. Sometimes we aim unrealistically high and at other times we are too modest and expect too little of ourselves. These guidelines will help you set goals and objectives correctly.*

323 Be clear about the difference between goals and objectives. Goals are more general, such as, "We are aiming to be the largest distributor in North America." Objectives are specifics that allow you to monitor performance very precisely. For example, "We aim to be the largest distributor in North America with sixty percent of the market by the end of 2013."

324 Meet with your associates to get them on board. Explain the importance of raising performance across the organization and the role they can play in this process. Stress the importance of goals and objectives, and get them involved in the choice of picking performance indicators, their goals, and plans to achieve these goals.

325 Create a measurement system to track success. Aim to have a balanced approach so all stakeholders benefit from your initiatives. Start with a review of your organization's mission. Identify the key elements that can be measured. For example, if your mission states, "We are committed to exceeding our customers' needs by providing high-quality products on time. This goal will enable us to satisfy our shareholders and provide an environment of security and growth for our staff," then the logical indicators of performance will come from the following categories:

✓ quality
✓ delivery
✓ shareholder's return
✓ staff security and growth

326 Ask for input regarding critical indicators of performance. As a guide, choose between four and eight indicators covering critical aspects of the mission.

327 Establish current performance levels by taking the average of the previous few months.

Set objectives with the input of staff. Ideally, objectives are SMART

✓ **S** pecific
✓ **M** easurable
✓ **A** greed-upon
✓ **R** easonable
✓ **T** ime-based

328 Set mini-objectives if goals are large so you can track changes each month. Smaller objectives allow you to celebrate successes more often. Each stepping stone should bring you closer to your final objective.

329 Benchmark your performance to assure yourself that your goals are both realistic and challenging. Compare your performance with other successful organizations or departments that have similar processes to yours. This way you not only will get a sense of what is possible, but you also will identify different practices that might apply to you and that would enhance your performance.

330 Develop action plans that will lead to improved performance. Ask for your people's input. List all the actions, together with dates, by which they must be completed. Ask for volunteers to undertake the tasks.

331 If your staff seems reluctant to take on the additional responsibility and involvement, then volunteer to help. Find out what might be impeding them. Remove any obstacles that your people identify.

332 Delegate jobs to specific people. Saying "Mark, you would do X?" will get a better response than "Who would like to do Y?"

333 Get agreement from your associates to spread the workload. Have them undertake some tasks such as data collection and research on a rotating basis.

334 Display your measurement and objectives goals where they can be easily viewed.

335 Review performance regularly. Compare it with the objectives. If performance is improving, praise those responsible. Also, learn from the positive changes made and ensure that they are repeated so performance does not slip. If performance is not improving, find out why. Involve your people in adjusting goals to a more realistic level, or better still, find new ways to achieve your existing goals.

How to...
Be a great mentor

Mentoring is about giving gifts – gifts of confidence, encouragement, and respect.

– ELIZABETH HOYLE

***M**entoring is a process focused* on the development of one person by another – typically not the employee's boss. Through regular contacts, the mentor guides and nurtures the associate (sometimes called the protégé or mentee) toward an agreed-upon goal. This process will enable the protégé to make a greater contribution to the organization.

While the premise on which mentoring is based is excellent, research suggests that fewer than fifty percent of the relationships tend to be successful. Mentors can do a number of things to strengthen the relationship and help their mentee avoid failure and disillusionment.

336 As a mentor, consider these actions before starting a mentoring relationship. Ask yourself:

✓ What do I know about the protégé?

✓ Is this someone I care to invest my time in?

✓ Do I know what their goals are?

✓ Is this something I have knowledge about?

✓ Am I willing to make the time to meet with this person regularly?

✓ Is my personality respectful of others, enabling me to be a patient listener and allow the protégé to find their own way?

337 Find out if your organization has a mentoring program. If it does, and it has been well designed, use it to

✓ make sure you are well matched with your protégé – their goals are areas of interest to you and are matters in which you have some expertise
✓ get the tools – forms, systems, and training – you need to manage the process
✓ get ongoing support as needed

338 Mentoring does not come easily or naturally to most people. So, take advantage of training programs that will give you the tools to

✓ get the process started on the right foot
✓ set goals with your protégé
✓ help your protégé develop a training plan that is compatible with their learning needs and style
✓ assist the protégé to identify their own solutions to problems
✓ give effective feedback to the protégé
✓ know when and how to bring the relationship to a happy conclusion

339 Encourage your protégé to get suitable training before you begin. This training will help them to

✓ understand and temper their expectations of how they will benefit
✓ become a full partner in the process
✓ set their own goals for the relationship
✓ understand their role and responsibilities
✓ give you constructive feedback if the relationship is not meeting their needs

340 When you're ready to start the process formally, set up your first meeting. Typically meetings are held monthly unless there is a rush for knowledge transfer to take place. Your first meeting should be to

- ✓ get to know each other
- ✓ clarify the objectives for the relationship
- ✓ estimate how long the process is likely to take
- ✓ decide how often you will meet
- ✓ decide where you will meet
- ✓ set up ground rules for the relationship. Typically these include:
  - maintaining a focus for each meeting
  - making meetings a priority by not cancelling unless there is a really good reason
  - maintaining confidentiality
  - respecting each other's ideas, even though you may not always agree
  - keeping an open mind in discussing issues
  - listening to and respecting each other

341 Maintaining a relationship that is mutually beneficial and rewarding is not easy. Consider these actions to increase your probability of success:

- ✓ Always greet your protégé warmly. Give them the sense that you value and look forward to your time together.
- ✓ Ensure that each meeting has clear objectives.
- ✓ Follow up on previously agreed-upon goals and action items.
- ✓ Deal with new items systematically, one at a time.
- ✓ Ensure that each decision taken is recorded in an action plan, together with a date by which it will be completed.

342 Make progress in helping your protégé move toward their goals. This is best achieved by

- ✓ spending most of your time listening. This will demonstrate your interest in the protégé's agenda rather than your own. Show your interest by

- leaning forward
- smiling
- maintaining eye contact
- making notes, if appropriate
- summarizing to ensure that you have captured the protégé's ideas and sentiments

✓ Show confidence in the protégé by allowing them time to solve their own problems. If they have not resolved the issue, ask open-ended questions that will guide them toward a solution. Examples include:
- What's the biggest issue?
- What would be your best approach?
- What would it look like if the matter was resolved?
- What's getting in your way of dealing with the issue?

✓ If you are unable to get an opinion from your protégé, give them some alternatives. Then ask them which one would be the most appealing and why. This will help them develop their self-confidence and problem-solving abilities.

✓ Help the protégé to see solutions by telling them a related story based on your own experience. Give them a chance to see parallel opportunities and solutions.

✓ When all else fails and your protégé seems unable to resolve an issue, ask for permission to make a suggestion. Asking for permission demonstrates your humility and gives the protégé one last chance to suggest their own ideas – which is always preferable to providing yours.

✓ Confirm whether your protégé has discovered a solution and summarize it to ensure that there is a specific action and time line for implementation.

343 Learn from your protégé. These associates are often younger than you; they probably come from a different value system and have a different skill set than you. This will give you added understanding and appreciation of the individual and others from their generation. Typically, protégés are chosen from the best and brightest in the organization. They have been in school more recently than you and therefore may have new ideas that you can benefit from.

344 When you feel your protégé's goals have been achieved and the meetings are becoming more social than beneficial, it might be time to formally wind up the relationship. This does not mean the two of you cannot maintain contact. You can meet informally for as long as both of you feel the time is well spent and beneficial. You will know the time is drawing near when

✓ the meetings are getting shorter
✓ there is less and less to discuss
✓ the discussions are becoming less focused

345 Celebrate the achievements of the relationship by

✓ informing Human Resources that you will not be meeting formally any longer
✓ inviting your protégé to give you formal feedback, evaluating what worked well for them and what recommendations they have for improvement
✓ having a meal together so you can toast your mutual achievements
✓ writing a letter to the protégé recording your satisfaction in the process and complimenting them on their achievements. Also let them know how you have benefited from the relationship

How to...
Conduct great performance reviews

Feedback is the breakfast of champions.

– KEN BLANCHARD

*T*he objective of an effective performance review *is to improve future performance more than it is to be a review of past performance. So, the process, done typically only annually in most organizations, is very important to the associate. It can have a very detrimental impact on the associate's confidence or motivation if done poorly, but could be highly motivating if done correctly.*

Ideally, a performance review should be a collaborative exercise conducted in a way that engages of the associate so they feel as if they "own" the plan moving forward.

Preparation

346 Preparation is essential. An effective performance-review process requires time and effort all year, not just before it takes place. So, during the period between appraisals, make sure you

✓ regularly update the associate's file so you are able to substantiate comments, good or bad, if necessary

✓ regularly give feedback whenever the associate exceeds

or fails to meet your performance expectations. This openness and honestly will ensure that there are no unpleasant surprises during the review

347 Set up a meeting time with your associate. Give them enough time to prepare their responses to the same performance criteria as yours.

348 Give the associate a sample questionnaire that allows them to do some focused thinking about the process and content of the interview. This will reduce the probability of surprises and give them a chance to complete the appropriate form from their perspective.

349 Don't schedule the meeting for a Friday, especially if a performance problem is going to be discussed. It may send the associate off to a lousy weekend. Earlier in the week is better, to give them time on the job to consider the issues and approach you for further clarification if necessary.

350 Allocate sufficient time for the meeting so it doesn't seem rushed. Typically, two hours will allow for a full interchange of ideas.

351 Make sure your documentation is prepared. Review the file so you're familiar with the content, especially

- ✓ the previous performance goals
- ✓ the collective agreement (if appropriate)
- ✓ the job description
- ✓ special achievements
- ✓ problems since the last appraisal

352 In your preparation, identify new projects, goals, and standards that should be achieved during the next period. Be prepared to handle unrealistic goals from your associate or those you cannot support.

Conducting the Appraisal

353 Set the climate for a productive interchange. Set the meeting room up so you can sit together instead of on opposite sides of the desk. Welcome the employee with a smile and a warm handshake.

354 Sit in a comfortable position next to the employee so you are close enough to suggest a positive climate but not so close as to make the employee uncomfortable. This will improve communication.

355 Set the ground rules for the meeting. These may include the importance of being

✓ open
✓ frank
✓ factual whenever possible
✓ positive
✓ future-focused

356 Ask the associate if they have any concerns about the process. Respond openly and honestly.

357 Review the associate's job. You may find the reality of the associate's performance is different from your ideas about the nature of the job's responsibilities. Priorities may have changed. Or maybe your associate's skill set now allows new opportunities for growth, challenges, and greater responsibility.

358 Review the goals that were set previously. Have they been achieved? If not, why not? Did the associate fail to meet some problems or were there issues that were beyond the associate's control?

359 Review the associate's achievements. Refer to your file. Also, ask about areas where the employee has felt they were particularly effective. Focus more on the narrative parts of the evaluation than on the numerical ratings.

360 Review areas where improvement is needed. Be specific about your concerns. Give examples to illustrate your knowledge and understanding of the issue.

361 Keep the process professional but relaxed by

- ✓ letting the associate do most of the talking
- ✓ listening to the associate's ideas
- ✓ being prepared to suggest solutions to problems and development needs but letting the associate contribute first
- ✓ not teaching, preaching, arguing, or defending your authority
- ✓ recognizing positive performance and identifying and dealing with problems
- ✓ supporting the associate's ideas rather than forcing your own
- ✓ inviting alternatives rather than assuming there is only one way to approach an issue
- ✓ using open-ended, reflective, and directive questions to stimulate discussion
- ✓ being specific and descriptive when expressing a concern about performance
- ✓ demonstrating to the associate that you want them to succeed

362 If your system calls for it, give your overall rating of the employee. If your discussions to this point have been open, frank, and factual, the final rating should be no surprise. If the associate seems upset or discouraged, express your desire to see a better review in the future and the steps they will take to make sure of it. Express your support for them so they don't feel as if they have been set up for failure.

363 Plan for improvement. Be positive. Ask for ideas to improve weaknesses. If the associate struggles to identify appropriate solutions, suggest some of your own. Gain commitment. Set an action plan to ensure that weaknesses are dealt with so the next steps are crystal clear.

364 Discuss the associate's goals and career aspirations. Be honest. Don't make promises that are hard to keep. Opportunities for advancement are all too few in organizations that are downsizing. Focus on development, personal growth, and providing opportunities to undertake important new projects should this be appropriate.

365 Before wrapping up, ask for feedback about the process. Is the associate satisfied? Has the meeting met their objectives?

366 Finally, summarize the key points of the appraisal and close the meeting on a positive note. Give a copy of the appraisal to the associate.

367 After each review, evaluate your own performance by asking the associate about their satisfaction with the process. Consider areas for improvement so you can get closer to perfection the next time around.

Follow Up

368 Hold regular formal and informal meetings with your associate to ensure that action plans for improvement are being implemented. Recognize special achievements. If the employee is not living up to commitments, find out why and help them get back on track. If they don't respond, follow your organization's disciplinary policy until the matter is resolved one way or the other.

How to...
Recognize employees

One of my bosses had a way of saying nice things about his workers that got back to them. True things, but nice things. We appreciated it, and we couldn't keep from trying to do more things that he could tell others about. People will work hard to uphold a good reputation.

– Fred Smith

Climate surveys reveal *that most employees don't feel appreciated and are seldom told when they do a good job. These same people typically complain that they get instant feedback when they make a mistake. This approach seems unfair and demotivating.*

Effective recognition is a challenge. In fact it's a minefield. Baby Boomers, while always happy to receive recognition, expect less of it than Generation Y associates. Working in a union shop adds complexity to the situation because you cannot reward one individual more than another. Furthermore, rewarding in tangible ways is taboo unless everyone is equally rewarded – which of course negates the value of recognition for something specific.

Here's how you can rectify the situation:

369 Make a distinction between rewards and recognition. Rewards are the benefits given to employees for specific achievements – their own, their team's, or the organization's.

Recognition consists of rewards given by individual supervisors to their people for superior performance. The recognition is usually spontaneous.

370 Designing a reward system is tricky, to say the least, especially when money is concerned. In doing so,

✓ reward teams as much as you do individuals. This will encourage collaborative behavior
✓ recognize your individual stars, but do so less publicly

371 Involve your employees in the design of a reward system. It's going to be impossible to please everyone, but widespread involvement will ensure that your system is

✓ acceptable to most
✓ relevant (rewards should include items, both cash and non-cash, that will be regarded as useful)
✓ fair (there is nothing worse than a system that is seen to be inequitable)

372 Increase the potency of your employees' recognition by

✓ demonstrating the types of recognition you value yourself
✓ doing so spontaneously
✓ including flexibility for managers by giving them a budget and discretion for recognition

373 In providing recognition to employees, you should

✓ avoid giving rewards for things that are already being done effectively
✓ reward only superior performance
✓ focus more on actions over and above the normal routine
✓ let associates know specifically why they are being rewarded.

374 Avoid patronizing when giving verbal recognition. People will know you are not being genuine when you

✓ exaggerate the extent of their achievement

✓ use a tone of voice or gestures inconsistent with your verbal message

✓ stretch the truth by using overblown language such as "always," "never," or "phenomenal" to describe performance that is only just above average

375 Avoid giving too much recognition and setting your employees up to depend on you for praise. Employees may become bereft of intrinsic motivation and will come to rely on you for assurance. Like a drug, if this assurance is withdrawn, it can become a real demotivator.

376 Constant or too frequent recognition can also become a problem if it discourages innovation by rewarding the same behaviors, so when it is not given, it demotivates them.

377 Relate rewards to job performance rather than to factors like seniority that have little to do with effort and skill.

378 Set goals or standards with your people individually and in teams. These should be specific, measurable, reasonable, yet challenging. With clear goals, you have benchmarks to recognize associates for. Any time they exceed the agreed-upon objective, you have the opportunity to acknowledge their effort and the result. Similarly, if individuals or your team are falling behind in achieving their goals, then make an effort to get back on track, you are presented with an opportunity to recognize their effort.

379 Everyone is different. So, getting to know your associates will allow you to personalize the recognition. Treat each person individually but equally. For example, don't reward one person with a pat on the back and another with a day off work for similar achievements.

380 Recognize employees immediately so there is a clear link between performance and reward.

381 Never let excellent work go unnoticed. When you catch people exceeding your expectations, make them aware of your appreciation and approval.

- ✓ Tell them soon after the positive behavior.
- ✓ Be specific about what it is that you appreciate. Saying "thank you for completing your report two days early" is better than "You're doing a great job."
- ✓ Let them know how you feel. Starting your praise with "I" will lead to a sharing of your feelings. "I'm delighted" or "I'm thrilled" are appropriate ways to begin.
- ✓ Do it intermittently. Giving praise all the time will appear patronizing especially if it is for the same thing and if you overdo the level of praise. So, provide praise spontaneously to maintain its value.
- ✓ Personalize the praise. Oral feedback costs nothing but is effective.

382 Vary the ways you recognize people so the process does not become predictable. There are literally hundreds of ways of showing appreciation. A few of the better ones include:

- ✓ a simple verbal thank you
- ✓ a written commendation, with a copy in the associate's file
- ✓ a personal note on a Post-it™ left on the associate's computer screen
- ✓ a gift
- ✓ time off
- ✓ a voucher to take their family out to a restaurant
- ✓ thanks, oral or written, from a senior manager
- ✓ praise in front of peers or at a management meeting
- ✓ praise in the newsletter
- ✓ a plaque
- ✓ an award at a banquet
- ✓ flowers sent to the associate's home

383 Periodically acknowledge people in front of their peers: It sends a clear message about what is important to you. Public recognition is appropriate for such things as an excellent

- ✓ team effort
- ✓ health and safety record
- ✓ attendance
- ✓ excessive overtime (send a letter of thanks to their family)

384 Don't overdo recognition. Constant compliments to staff will turn the process into a mockery.

385 Senior managers design reward systems. To be effective, they need to be linked to measurable results, organizational values, or core competencies. Key performance indicators typically relate to benefits for one or more of the stakeholders – customers, shareholders, and employees.

V

How to...
MANAGE EFFECTIVELY EVERY DAY

Lessons 386–715

How to...
Communicate with a diverse workforce

> *We are all unique, and if that is not fulfilled,*
> *then something wonderful has been lost.*
> *– Martha Graham*

*O*ur workforce is becoming *more diverse. Borders are porous and people around the world are migrating to economies that offer better futures for them and their families. Organizations today, especially in metropolitan areas, have a very different mix of people than they did fifty years ago. This presents an interesting challenge in terms of understanding cultural differences and nuances. But it also presents a wonderful opportunity. Appreciating and benefiting from this melting pot of talent may be key to success in your organization. So, here are some strategies that will improve your effectiveness.*

386 Check your attitude and comfort levels. Do you have prejudices against certain people? Are there some you value less than others? If so, you will have a hard time communicating effectively with people of other races and ethnic origins. It is important to judge associates based on their individual talents, knowledge, skills, and attitudes. Don't assume you already know what they are like based on stereotypical information.

387 Create workplace programs that allow associates to share their stories and experiences so employees get to know each other on a more personal level and can see their commonality rather than their differences. These programs can include diversity celebrations or potluck lunches where employees are encouraged to bring in traditional foods for others to taste.

388 Create buddy programs so people who may be new to the country can look to a veteran to show them the ropes.

389 Your communications with ethnically different people is very important.

✓ Be patient in dealing with people who are not fluent in your language. If you expect too much, too quickly, you will confuse and frustrate.

✓ Don't show anger if people don't understand at first. Try to project an understanding and sympathetic demeanor.

✓ If people speak English poorly but understand reasonably well, ask them to demonstrate their understanding through actions rather than words.

✓ Avoid jokes. Your humor will not be understood. Worse still, it may be seen as a joke at their expense.

✓ Speak slowly and clearly, but don't raise your voice.

✓ Use face-to-face communication whenever possible. Avoid telephone conversations.

✓ If you have complicated or long-winded instructions, break them into manageable steps.

✓ Use interpreters only if communications are impossible. Discourage people from becoming dependent on interpreters.

✓ Use pictures and diagrams instead of words. Back up oral directions with simple written instructions.

390 Don't assume that difficulty understanding means lack of intelligence. Many people doing menial jobs in their adopted country were teachers, engineers, lawyers, and medical practitioners in their native countries.

391 Encourage people to take English courses. Make time available for them to get to classes.

How to...
Gain commitment from project team members

We fail or succeed together. If we fail, no one is a winner.

– *ANONYMOUS*

Using interdisciplinary teams is commonplace today. In fact, the hallmark of a successful leader is having the ability to lead a diverse group of people to a project's successful conclusion, on time, and on budget. Your team will stand or fall depending on how committed members are to the goal. Your challenge as manager is to get that commitment, not from just one person, but from the whole team. This is how you do it:

392 Start well. Before starting any project, make sure the chemistry of the team is such that members are happy to work together to help each other. The right tone can be set if at the start of the project you

✓ meet to have everyone become acquainted
✓ identify to the group each member's special talents, so other members will value them
✓ create expectations as to how the team will work together. Include such things as
  • attending meetings on time
  • completing assignments on time
  • asking for help if a member hits a roadblock

- respecting and listening to each other at meetings

✓ stress the importance of the project and the benefits to the team of a successful outcome

393 Be prepared. Have a draft project plan for the team to review so expectations are clear. Have specific deliverables worked out for each stage of the project. If your team members don't know what you want, they won't know what to reach for. Ensure that the people responsible for deliverables have agreed to them.

394 Be enthusiastic. Your passion for a successful outcome will galvanize more energy than a project few have interest in. Also, be persuasive about the "boring stuff." Budgets and deadlines on their own will not fire anyone's imagination but tying them into the general vision of the project will make them compelling and will get your team more enthused about bringing the project in on time and under budget.

395 Be open. Encourage your team to make their concerns known to you directly or, if appropriate, at your meetings. By bringing issues into the open they can be addressed instead of remaining an undercurrent that will derail or slow down the project.

396 Be respectful. Understand that team members have other responsibilities and report to other managers. Respect their time. Don't hold meetings that have no purpose. Deal directly with members who may be falling behind without waiting for a meeting to address the issue.

397 Be open and flexible. If a member raises an issue or has a bright idea that isn't your own, thank them and include it without putting your own spin on it. This will give the team member a greater sense of ownership in the project.

398 Be understanding and empathetic. From time to time

schedule progress meetings. This will give you a chance to evaluate progress, identify roadblocks, solve problems, and make decisions. Without the enthusiasm of your team members these things won't happen. Gauge the level of enthusiasm not only from what is being said but also from what is left unsaid. If people start to clam up, you've either lost your team or something wasn't clear. Use humor to lighten the atmosphere and find out where the problem is. If you establish the right atmosphere, people will feel freer to voice their objections and suggestions, making buy-in stronger when these are addressed and resolved.

399 **Be concise**. People are busy and often impatient. Be prepared to get your message across quickly. Make it as easy to understand as possible without cluttering it up with irrelevant information.

400 **Follow up**. Make sure minutes are taken at all meetings and are circulated soon thereafter. Summarize expectations so actions are clear. Post a copy on the team bulletin board (if the project is within your department) so all team members can refer to it.

401 **Celebrate**. Share the joy that comes from success. If the team is running ahead in terms of time and budget let them know and celebrate appropriately. If the whole project is successful make sure brownie points are shared and that the team is given exposure to more senior leaders.

How to...
Communicate effectively in writing

Writing without thinking is like shooting without aiming.

– ARNOLD GLASGOW

*M*ost job descriptions include *a requirement for "effective communication skills, both oral and written." Sadly, many people find it difficult to express their ideas on paper and this hinders their ability to influence those higher in the organization.*

With people reading and sending dozens of e-mails each day, it has become critical to be able to express thoughts clearly and effectively. Here are some suggestions that will help you improve your writing skills:

402 Think before you write. Consider what you need to communicate and ask yourself whether it can best be done orally or verbally. The most important reasons for documentation are

✓ an important decision must be made
✓ you are dealing with a complex issue
✓ the materials must be studied before a decision is made

403 Write your material in a logical sequence so it flows and is easy to understand.

State the purpose of the communication at the beginning. Begin by letting the reader know the value of reading your note. Entice them with introductions such as "This report will reveal how the corporation can save up to $15,000,000!"

404 If the communication is lengthy, insert an executive summary at the beginning.

405 If action is required, let everyone who reads the document know what is expected of them.

406 Be brief and to the point – your key ideas should stand out clearly.

407 End the communication with a short summary. Tie it back to the opening paragraph containing your objective.

408 Give a positive spin to your message. For example, "Company policy requires that you do not smoke in the building" can be turned into a positive statement by saying, "You are welcome to smoke in the courtyard."

409 Show the reader how the benefits will affect them. Converting an "I" into a "you" can often do this. For example, "I know we can offer significant advantages over our competition" can be changed to "We would be pleased to demonstrate the benefits you will receive."

410 Let your readers know that you have a keen sense of their needs. This will motivate them to take the actions you require.

411 Keep paragraphs short, especially the first one. If the material looks easy to read, the recipients will get into the meat of the document before they know it. Vary the length of paragraphs throughout the piece, but try to keep all of them relatively short.

412 Avoid clogging your document with details. Save background and technical material for attachments or appendices. Alert your readers to their existence by referring to them: "See Attachment A."

413 Use plain language and avoid jargon unless it is part of your readers' normal vocabulary.

414 Avoid repetition. Draw attention to important ideas by varying how they are formatted and placed within the document.

415 Avoid gender bias in your writing. The following techniques are useful when dealing with the difficult "he/she" problem:

✓ Use plural subjects. For example, "The manager should meet regularly with his salesmen" could be expressed as "Managers should meet regularly with their salespeople."

✓ Use plural or neutral pronouns. For example, "No man is an island" could become "No one is an island" or "We are not islands."

✓ Use neutral nouns instead of singular pronouns. For example, "Ask him who knows" could become "Ask the person who knows."

✓ Avoid possessive pronouns. For example, "The manager should tell his people" could be expressed as "The manager should tell staff."

416 Write as if you are speaking with your colleagues. A conversational style is more approachable and readable than stilted, formal language.

417 Send copies to relevant people only. People who receive copies without expecting them will be confused and may suspect you of playing office politics.

418 Model your writing on excellent examples. Make copies of writing that impresses you and keep them on file.

419 Read your work aloud to see if it sounds right. Make changes if necessary and read aloud again until it works.

420 Before circulating any written or electronic document, ask yourself, as a reader, if the information is comprehensible and clear.

How to...
Listen to what is not being said (reading body language)

The most important thing in communicating is to hear what isn't being said.

– PETER F. DRUCKER

*R**eading body language** teaches you to listen with your eyes as well as your ears. Here are a few common indicators in Western culture – but keep in mind that other cultures have different signals. Get a colleague from that culture to teach them to you.*

Behavior	Likely Meaning
Arms or legs crossed	Closed to your ideas, unreceptive
Body: leaning back	Skeptical, unwilling to commit
Body: leaning back with hands behind head	Relaxed, possible reservations, no sense of urgency
Body: slouching	Taking cover, low self esteem
Eyes blinking slowly	Uncomfortable, unwilling to be there
Eyes at top left	Quickly evaluating, planning next move; possibly hostile

Behavior	Likely Meaning
Eyes at top right	Problem solving, trying to figure something out
Eyes darting	Anxious, unconfident, unprepared
Eyes looking over tops of glasses	Evaluating, assessing
Eyes narrowed	Evaluating, assessing, with possible skepticism
Eyes staring	Not paying attention, daydreaming
Eyes wide	Interested, making an important point
Hands at sides	Neutral
Hands clasped in back	Acknowledging authority, possibly something to hide
Hands clasped in front	Possibly conservative, with a closed mind
Hands on hips/hip jut	Confident, bordering on arrogant – issuing a challenge
Hands on table	Willing to get things done
Hands open, palms down	Demanding – showing control
Hands open, palms up	Asking, wanting, needing – showing vulnerability
Head cocked to one side	Listening with interest
Head straight on	Confident
Head tilted back	Arrogant, cocky
Head tilted down	Shy, ashamed, or lying
Jacket buttoned	Formal
Jacket unbuttoned	Informal
Smile with eyes crinkled	Joyful, expressing pleasure
Smile without eyes crinkled	Trying to gain approval

How to...
Manage the grapevine

*The single biggest problem in communication
is the illusion that it has taken place.*

— GEORGE BERNARD SHAW

Surveys show *that most people get the information they need
through the grapevine rather than official channels. Here's what
you can do to reduce the impact of distorted information:*

421 Prevent rumors from starting. When there is uncertainty in the organization due to changes in leadership, a merger, closing of offices, or a sharp decline in business, be ahead of the curve and feed as much information to staff as you can.

422 Take the attitude that it is better to give too much information than too little.

423 Hold regular briefings. These, by definition, should be short. They can be stand-up meetings in the office, cafeteria, or a huddle on the factory floor. If you don't have new information, encourage questions. These may uncover rumors you are not yet aware of.

424 Keep a flip chart or whiteboard in your work area. Write news on it regularly. Allow your people to record questions on it they want answered at the next meeting.

425 Deal with rumors right away.

426 Anticipate issues that might provoke negative gossip. Deal with them quickly.

427 Never deny or lie about the truth – your credibility will suffer and trust between you and your people will be jeopardized. Often information reaches your people before you get it. Try to track down the source and establish whether the information is truth or fiction. When you have the facts, let people have them right away.

428 Go to the source of the rumor. Find out if you or your team will be affected. Find ways to position yourself to take advantage of the situation. Develop a plan that will demonstrate how you and your people could help to make the change successful.

429 When you go to the source of a rumor, don't demand answers or put people on the spot. Make it easy for them to help you by asking questions that can be dealt with hypothetically. For example: "If, at some time in the future, there was a downsizing, which departments would be cut first?" Watch their body language when they answer so you can understand how they feel about the issue.

430 Maintain a positive attitude. Take particular care to do good work. As your colleagues' work productivity and attitudes deteriorate, yours will shine by comparison.

431 Watch for signs that rumors are becoming reality. Typically, senior managers will be

✓ spending more time in meetings
✓ looking harassed
✓ whispering among themselves
✓ retreating behind closed doors to take phone calls or hold discussions

432 Be open to change. Look at all the alternatives. Change brings opportunities. New directions should challenge and energize you.

How to...

Influence those above you in the chain of command

> *Strong beliefs win strong men,*
> *and then make them stronger.*
>
> – WALTER BAGEHOT

Being creative and having wonderful ideas *is of little value if you can't sell the ideas and have them implemented. Whenever you have a great idea, you need to sell it to the people with power to carry it out. Without their blessing, you will never get the green light.*

By following a few key principles you can make the higher-ups as keen on your ideas as you are.

Prepare

433 Prepare, prepare, prepare. Accumulate as much backup information as you can find. Make sure you have research that

- ✓ suggests that any spending will provide a ROI that will at least meet the minimum organizational criterion
- ✓ demonstrates that your idea has worked elsewhere under similar circumstances. The more novel or controversial your idea, the more supporting documentation you will need.
- ✓ is supported by key executives in the organization

434 Prepare the decision makers. Don't spring a big new idea on them without letting them know from time to time where your thinking and research are pointing you. As you get closer to the final sale, solicit ideas from the executive leaders so you can include their feedback in your presentation. If the focus of senior management is on cost cutting, emphasize how your idea will save money. If incorporating new technology and innovations is the hot topic in your company, emphasize those aspects. This will increase your chances of getting approval.

435 Prepare your presentation. Decide which presentation medium might work best. If it is to a group, then a formal presentation with PowerPoint™ slides may work well. But, if it is to a single individual, you may find paper-printed slides useful, presented in a flip file rather than as a computer-projected show.

436 Rehearse your presentation beforehand with a colleague, a friend in the same field, or your mentor. Remember to put together a written package to support your presentation and have your test audience review it.

437 Make sure your promises and predictions are realistic. Senior management can smell snake oil a mile off.

438 Prepare the logistics. If you're doing a formal presentation with a number of people, book the meeting room and get their commitment to attend as far in advance as possible. Make sure that you have the right equipment, that you are familiar with it, and that it works.

Present Like a Pro

439 When executives enter the room, greet them warmly. Hold the hand you shake a second longer than usual, shake firmly, and smile with your whole face.

440 Project optimism. Ideas delivered cheerfully get more buy-in than those delivered in a gloomy Chicken Little manner.

441 Be brief and to the point. Senior managers operate under severe time constraints, and their attention spans can be quite limited. If you have a lot of supporting documentation, make a handout to go with your presentation.

442 Listen to and show interest in their reactions, and respond to their concerns. This will show the importance you place on their opinions.

443 Give compliments to good questions and constructive comments. Genuine compliments, especially those on topic with your idea, will warm your audience to you and encourage further interaction.

444 If you don't get immediate buy-in, determine the objections and request a follow-up meeting at which you can address them. Don't whine.

Follow Up

445 As soon as possible, send out a memo to thank those who attended your presentation. The memo should address the main issues raised at the presentation and indicate your determination to deal with them immediately.

446 Gather information about any outstanding concerns regarding implementation or approval, conditional or otherwise. Reflect these thoughts and decisions in a final short report to senior management, describing conclusions and next steps. Don't let the idea rest until a decision is made.

How to...
Communicate one-on-one

*Wisdom is the reward you get for a lifetime
of listening when you'd have preferred to talk.*

– DOUG LARSON

*T*he greatest mistake *leaders can make is to assume that their
employees believe them, agree with them, or understand them.
Communication problems happen all the time. But, with a little
care and attention, many of these breakdowns can be avoided.*

*We typically speak at between one hundred and two hundred
words per minute, yet we are able to listen at many times that
rate. But we find it difficult to have a meaningful conversation
when the phone is ringing, e-mails are coming through, and
others are trying to get our attention all at the same time. Our
ability to focus becomes compromised and it takes an enormous
amount of energy and effort to listen to and receive a message
clearly.*

447 The purpose of communicating is to gather information, give
direction, show empathy, solve problems, make decisions,
give encouragement, and share ideas.

448 There are many barriers preventing your message from
getting through to the receiver. These can lead to delays,
errors, and frustration. Being aware of them is the first step
to overcoming them. These barriers include

✓ *Noise.* Many workplaces are noisy because of machines, conversations, and outside traffic. We often have to wear earplugs to reduce the levels of noise. This makes it incredibly challenging to hold a conversation without shouting. Often the solution is to find a quiet spot or a quieter time, especially if the conversation is going to be protracted. If those options are unavailable, you will simply have to shout. Make sure you constantly summarize what you are hearing back to your conversation partner to help prevent miscommunication.

✓ *Cultural differences.* Workplaces are more multicultural than ever, especially in major metropolitan areas. It is not uncommon to find people from a dozen or more different backgrounds in a single organization. This presents an enormous challenge to anyone wanting to communicate effectively with everyone, as personal style invariably creeps into the process. It is necessary to maintain an objective, bias-neutral approach to each person, while at the same time making allowances for that person's culture.

✓ *Perceptions.* Our understanding and interpretation of messages may be clouded by internal factors. Our minds filter information differently depending on the level of stress we are under, as well as the values, knowledge, and experience we bring to the information being communicated

✓ *Typecasting.* Often we develop a schema, or mental pattern, that can taint our ability to communicate effectively. For example, if we typecast tech employees as laid-back, human resources people as soft, design employees as flaky, or accountants as repressed bean-counters, we may be tempted to avoid challenging them with tasks outside their perceived spheres of interest or consulting them on issues outside their areas of expertise. However, many of the best ideas come from people who can see challenges from an outside, neutral perspective.

449 The most effective way to overcome obstacles to effective communication is to listen actively. Listening is far more difficult than it appears. People who listen with purpose typically

- ✓ spend less time talking
- ✓ listen to be influenced rather than to rebut ideas
- ✓ rarely start their sentences with "but"
- ✓ understand any biases they have and work consciously to overcome them
- ✓ ask more open-ended questions
- ✓ make notes so they have all the details
- ✓ paraphrase often to confirm understanding and show that they have captured the essence of what has been communicated
- ✓ do not finish other people's sentences

450 Give feedback. There is no point in having the other person guess how you feel about their idea. Let them know. But do so professionally, especially if you have reservations about the idea. Focus on the issue, explaining specifically what you object to. Never make it personal. Demonstrate that you care about the other's input, but that you have a problem with the idea. Ask for other ideas or different ways of modifying the idea to meet your criteria.

451 One of the most effective ways to demonstrate listening is to pay attention to what is meant rather than to what is being said. Meaning is often conveyed through nonverbal means such as body language. Studies suggest that as much as eighty percent of communication is nonverbal, so to ignore this aspect is to miss most of the message. Pay attention to a person's

- ✓ *Eyes*. It is said that eyes are windows to the soul. Breaking eye contact or staring blankly may indicate a lack of interest in the conversation.

- ✓ *Facial expression*. A receptive listener will smile with warmth in their eyes. A smile indicates caring, empathy, and enthusiasm.

✓ *Voice modulation.* A quiet voice can indicate indecisiveness or uncertainty although this can vary from culture to culture.

✓ *Proximity and posture.* The way people position themselves relative to you will indicate their interest in what you have to say. Standing closer, rather than farther away, facing you and leaning slightly forward all demonstrate their interest in the discussion. However, cultural background may affect personal distancing during a conversation.

How to...
Communicate with your team

*So much of what we call management
is making it difficult for people to work.*

– Peter Drucker

*A*ny survey of unfulfilled needs in an organization will reveal inadequate communications. Communicating with employees is like filling a bottomless pit – there can never be too much.

Followers judge their leaders primarily by the quantity and quality of their communications.

452 Opportunities to communicate include

✓ informal interactions, such as conversations while walking around
✓ formal interaction at meetings
✓ presentations at employee information sessions
✓ presentations to stakeholders, such as suppliers, shareholders, or the board, aimed at winning support for change or a new project

453 Time is money. Taking people away from their work for group meetings and information sessions is expensive. Leaders need to focus their communications on key issues that affect the performance of the organization and deal with issues of importance to their people. Typically these are

✓ explaining the direction of the organization

✓ sharing strategies that will be used to achieve success
✓ letting people know the role they can play in achieving company goals
✓ updating employees on how the organization is doing and, more specifically, how their area is performing
✓ providing recognition when appropriate

454 Before holding a communications meeting with employees, ask yourself the following questions:

✓ *How often* should we hold these meetings? Monthly would be nice, but is it practical? Does our environment change so quickly that we need to bring everyone up to speed so frequently? Are there other ways of communicating important information in a way everyone will understand?

✓ *What* information should I be sharing? How detailed should it be? How confidential is that information? More is better, for sure, and sharing confidential information does send a message that people can be trusted and are partners in the business.

✓ *Who* should be invited? Should all the employees meet together or should they be separated so they get levels of information customized for their area's needs? For example, salespeople may need different information than operations employees.

✓ *Who* should present in a company-wide meeting? All senior managers should be involved in presenting their part of the big picture from a variety of perspectives. However, if some of them have a problem being succinct and will take away from the time of others, it may be best to have one person do the entire show.

✓ *Why* have the meetings? This is a no-brainer. Your employees deserve and need to know what's going on, how you're doing, what the future holds for them, and how anticipated changes may affect their work.

✓ *Where* should you hold the meeting? Meeting rooms are often too small to hold a general town-hall type meeting. The cafeteria is one alternative, as it is usually big enough to hold most of the employees, although the ambiance is not particularly conducive to a serious meeting. Be sure to use the room that will have the fewest distractions and the lowest level of interfering noise.

455 At the meeting, ensure that you get the biggest bang for your buck by

✓ keeping the presentation as short as is practical. Remember, most adults have a seven-minute attention span. So, if the meeting goes beyond a few minutes, be sure to change the pace, make it interesting, and keep it interactive. Moving onto new topics in quick succession will also maintain attention.
✓ providing highlights without getting into too much depth, unless questions require it
✓ making sure you are talking at the level of your audience
✓ presenting the information in a way that indicates your understanding of the needs of the audience
✓ walking around the room to ensure that you make eye contact with as many people as possible
✓ encouraging questions, especially if you know the issue being covered is a sensitive one
✓ speaking slowly and clearly, especially if the audience is multilingual
✓ complementing your presentation with PowerPoint™ slides and using graphs and pictures that strengthen the written words
✓ using the words "we" and "us," suggesting that everyone is in the same boat. Using "me" and "you" suggests that you value the hierarchy and that you are different – perhaps better – than your audience.

456 If you are dealing with a subject that may evoke some resistance, be prepared to reduce push-back by

- ✓ balancing your presentation with a mixture of facts and emotions. Too much of either could sour the message. A good message tugs at the heart of your audience while at the same time providing factual information.
- ✓ involving the audience. Try to engage their five senses so they feel actively involved. This will create a more relaxed and receptive atmosphere.
- ✓ "stroking" the audience. Let them know that you appreciate their support, loyalty, and efforts. This will reinforce their commitment to the behavior.
- ✓ focusing on benefits before strategies. Let people know how they will be affected and the rewards for getting on board. The details can be shared later, when people are receptive to the change.
- ✓ knowing who your opinion leaders are and doing whatever you can to get them on board before you share your message. They will be less likely to criticize it publicly if they already understand it.
- ✓ showing examples of similar plans that have worked elsewhere. This will increase confidence that your plan has a good chance of success.
- ✓ running your ideas by some of the toughest critics in advance. Listen intently to their criticisms and ensure that you are able to deal with them.
- ✓ invoking the past, citing similar struggles that had positive results.

457 If people ask questions, handle them with care. Demonstrate your interest by

- ✓ repeating the question in your own words to be sure you have understood and to let others who may not have heard the question know the issue
- ✓ showing no annoyance if the question is challenging. Demonstrate your class by focusing on the issue and not the person. Never roll your eyes or show frustration; focus on the objection raised. At the end of your explanation get confirmation that the question has been answered satisfactorily and your answer understood.

How to...
Make decisions

Nothing is more difficult, and therefore more precious, than to be able to decide.

– NAPOLEON BONAPARTE

Researchers agree that most important decisions are not made on the basis of logic. Most are based on emotions. Little wonder therefore that most people buy stocks at the top of the market and sell them at the bottom. Having a system and knowing when – and when not – to involve others will help improve decision making. Here are some general principles:

458 Understand that there are many ways to make decisions. Most commonly, decisions can be made by

  ✓ minority. One person or a few people make the decision for others.
  ✓ majority. The decision is made based on fifty-one percent or more by vote.
  ✓ consensus. The decision is made with the agreement and support of everyone involved.

459 Understand which decision-making methods are appropriate for each situation.

  ✓ Decisions by a minority are appropriate when
    • there is lack of time

- there is an emergency
- the issue relates to health and safety
- the decision is strategic
- one person is the acknowledged expert.

✓ The majority opinion should be used to make decisions when
  - a decision is required quickly
  - there are too many people to negotiate a consensus
  - the issue is very divisive
  - it is desirable to get buy-in from as many people as possible

460 Decisions that affect your associates and require their commitment should ideally be made by consensus. If you want your team to reach a consensus, hold a meeting at which you will give the opportunity to explore a number of ideas before finally narrowing them down to one the group finds best and most acceptable.

461 You will be more likely to achieve a consensus by following the *Nominal Group Technique* process. This process consists of eight critical steps:

✓ Agree on the goal. "Can we agree to reach a consensus on X?"

✓ Agree on the process. Ask participants if they will support the majority. Any other constraints should also be agreed to. "Can we all agree to support the majority? Are there any choices that we might not be able to live with?"

✓ Have participants generate their own ideas if they do not already have some.

✓ Collect ideas by round robin. Each member in turn gives an idea and these are recorded where everyone can see them without discussion or criticism.

✓ Clarify and lobby. Key ideas are evaluated in greater detail. If you have a long list, vote to narrow it to the top five. Next, spend time evaluating the pros and cons of each idea.

✓ Take a vote. Participants make their choices by

- voting as many times as they like
- having a weighted vote (giving everyone three votes, the first choice getting five points, the second getting three points, and the third getting one point).

✓ Tally the votes and identify the top choice(s).

✓ Check for consensus. The leader checks to see if everyone can support the most popular choice. "Can we all live with this choice?"

462 Sometimes one individual may choose not to live with the rest. It is possible that they were not given a chance to lobby. If that is the case, give them that opportunity and take a revote. If, after the revote, they are still dissenting, then you will have to work with the majority vote. If the same person objects frequently, there may be an underlying issue why they refuse to accept the process. There may be a performance issue that is best dealt with outside of the meeting.

463 For more complex decisions, you could use a matrix or tally sheet (see below) to arrive at the most popular choice. The value of this system is that it incorporates a number of well-defined criteria of the ideal choice.

✓ Allow each person to evaluate each idea by ranking it in terms of the agreed-to criteria. Collect the sheets and create a master tally sheet.

✓ Use the tally sheet for Step 6 of the *Nominal Group Technique*. It's important that people agree in advance to support the majority and that they confirm their support when the most popular choice is declared.

Criteria	Issue					
	1	**2**	**3**	**4**	**5**	**6**
Value Added						
Desirable						
Measurable						
Control						
Simple						
Payback						
Repeated often						
Other						
Total						

Score: 1, 2, or 3
1 = Low (Poorest)   2 = Moderate (Average)   3 = High (Best)

The Item with the Highest Score Is:

How to...
Learn to improve from an exit interview

The best morale exists when you never hear the word mentioned. When you hear a lot of talk about it, it's usually lousy.

– DWIGHT D. EISENHOWER

*R**arely is a manager happy** when a star employee leaves the company. However, you can turn a negative into a positive by learning their reasons. It may help you prevent other contributors from heading for the exit. Conducting an exit interview will also give valuable insights into those aspects of your corporate culture that need improvement.*

Before Your Associate Leaves

464 Mention that you would value any opinions and insights into the working conditions at your company that could be useful to you as a manager.

465 Offer to set up an interview with a human resources employee if your associate would prefer to be interviewed by someone else.

466 Emphasize that all information will be kept confidential.

467 Schedule the interview during their last week of employment.

468 Be sensitive to the venue you choose and consult your departing colleague as to where they would feel most comfortable holding the interview. Long-term employees often prefer exit luncheons outside the office. In any case, choose somewhere neutral to mitigate the "boss-subordinate" feeling.

At the Interview

469 Place your associate at ease by sitting adjacent to them at a four-person table rather than directly across from them.

470 Remember that you are there to listen and gather information, not to defend yourself. Take open notes. Paraphrase the occasional comment to demonstrate that you are genuinely trying to understand.

471 Encourage your associate to be specific. Ask open-ended questions about their perceptions of your leadership style, team, or departmental interaction with management at all levels. Ask how obstacles, difficulties on the job, or the corporate culture as a whole affected their job performance or job satisfaction. Ask if there is any other information they feel you need to know.

472 Use your associate's new job as a tool to determine what working conditions at your company need improvement. Find out about salary and benefits, the new work environment, what generally attracted them to this new position. If they are leaving without a new position lined up, this could mean either that there are compelling personal reasons or that the work environment had become intolerable. Try to elicit this information without being aggressive or patronizing.

473 Thank your associate for their time and willingness to help you make your company a better place to work. Sincerely congratulate them and wish them the best of luck.

474 Here are some pointed questions that will enhance the effectiveness of the meeting:

- ✓ If you had my job, what would you change first? Why?
- ✓ How could I improve our work area?
- ✓ What frustrated you most about the job?
- ✓ What did you like best about the job?
- ✓ What corporate policies do you feel are most praiseworthy?
- ✓ What corporate policies and procedures made your work life difficult? Why?
- ✓ What will your new job give you that we have not?
- ✓ What will you miss most about working here?
- ✓ If you could tell the president one thing, what would it be?
- ✓ What should we be doing to ensure that your replacement stays with us?

After Your Employee Has Left

475 Organize your information in point form and pass on the most urgent problems to those who can take responsibility to fix them. Reflect on your colleague's assessment of your performance and adjust accordingly.

476 If information from the interview points to a severe or widespread problem within the department, arrange a follow-up interview with your former associate a few weeks later. Their point of view may have altered once they left the organization, or their opinions may have clarified with time. Again, ask if they would prefer a human resources person as a more objective interviewer.

How to...
Give critical feedback

*It's always worthwhile to make
others aware of their worth.*

– MALCOLM FORBES

*The most important skill in a manager's repertoire is
the ability to communicate effectively to associates about their
performance, whether their performance is positive or negative.
Often, managers fail to deal with this issue altogether, thereby
condoning poor performance and frustrating those who put in
extra effort to compensate for it. Positive and negative feedback
are two sides of the same coin. Both must be delivered in a professional, forthright manner to ensure maximum effect.*

477 Critical Feedback is something most of us hate giving.
It's difficult and, if not done correctly, can lead to morale
problems.

478 Immediacy is essential – always deliver feedback as close to
the event in question as possible. This enables you to either
nip a problem in the bud or to demonstrate your appreciation of excellence.

479 Make an appointment with your associate to discuss their
performance in private. It is essential that they feel like a
participant rather than a subject. Don't be afraid to be assertive if they seem unwilling to discuss their performance.

480 Get an invitation to give the feedback. Say "I'd like to discuss the issue with you. Is that OK?" Few people will refuse an opportunity to deal with and remove a stressful situation. And, having accepted your invitation to discuss the issue, your associate will be more open to resolving it.

481 Be clear and concise in expressing what you find unacceptable. Providing explicit details of a problem (dates, places, numbers) will avoid giving the impression of a personal attack. Always focus on the specific issue, and avoid sweeping generalizations as to the person's character or work habits. Make it clear that this is an issue of performance, not personality.

482 Relate the problem to the larger goals and standards of your company, and be sure that your employee understands the connection. You are not being patronizing – you are treating your associate as an essential participant in the future of the company.

483 Confine your comments to areas and issues your associate can control – if part of the blame or achievement lies elsewhere, acknowledge this.

484 Choose your words carefully. Avoid vague generalizations, inflammatory language, and exaggerations ("You always do this sort of thing").

485 Be specific. Indicate exactly what you are unhappy about ("I'm disappointed that the report was ten days late").

486 Be assertive. Focus on the issue, not the person. Let them know your feelings by using "I" statements whenever possible ("I'm upset because this report does not include the figures we agreed upon"). Speak with a firm voice and maintain eye contact.

487 Involve your associate in planning for changed behavior based on this discussion – any solution or continuation of excellence should be seen as a joint venture. Develop a "contract" – either written or spoken – and agree to the terms and to a date by which the provisions of the understanding will be fulfilled. The contract should outline key discussion points and the outcomes you have agreed upon. Make sure you both are clear on the meaning of each statement in the contract. Say, as often as necessary: "What I understand this to mean is X. Do we agree on this?"

488 Confirm a date for a future meeting to assess the success of the contract. Be clear that you view this as an ongoing process and are paying attention. You will not forget about this, and neither should your associate.

489 Each time you need to give negative feedback, run through the following checklist:

✓ Get agreement to deal with the issue.

✓ Make an appointment for a private discussion.

✓ State the facts.

✓ Confirm that the issue is a problem.

✓ Determine the cause.

✓ Ask for a solution. Listen and probe for an acceptable solution.

✓ Determine the next step.

✓ Document your understanding, especially if there are multiple items. Agree on all points and the time line for implementation.

✓ Set a time for the next appointment.

How to...
Orient new staff

You never get a second chance to make a first impression.

*H*aving hired the right people, *you can promote their successful adjustment into the organization by orienting them properly. This is a task in which both you and your associates ensure that the new associate is exposed to a large number of people who will jointly take responsibility for their seamless and successful introduction to the organization.*

Before the Arrival of the New Associate

490 Plan to ensure a successful integration of the new person.

- ✓ At a staff meeting, inform your associates about the new member of staff and your expectations of their roles in the person's successful induction to the organization.

- ✓ Have the new hire's work station set up with supplies.

- ✓ Have someone greet the new employee on arrival.

- ✓ Post a letter on the bulletin board and e-mail all those with whom the new associate will come into contact, welcoming the employee and inviting others to do the same. The communication should also contain some information about the new hire.

The First Day

491 Spend some one-on-one time getting to know the new associate better. If you weren't involved in their hiring, learn about their work background, previous jobs, special skills, likes, and dislikes.

492 Give the new associate documentation on salary and benefits. Spend time on the benefits so they can see the value of their entire package.

493 Give the new employee a tour of the operations. Show them the key facilities, including parking, washrooms, the cafeteria, and emergency exits. Tour the different departments, discuss how they interact, and how they relate to yours. Also show/demonstrate the major products and services. Information will give people the big picture so they can see how they fit into it.

494 Review the company's vision, mission, and values. Also, share your management philosophies so they understand the type of working culture you are trying to create and the type of actions that will make them into a star.

495 Discuss how the employee can contribute to the successful achievement of corporate goals.

496 While you can do some of the orientation, consider involving someone else. Linking the new associate with a person from another work area can be beneficial in that it

- ✓ suggests that departments work together
- ✓ stresses teamwork
- ✓ establishes contacts with people in other areas
- ✓ improves communications between work areas
- ✓ demonstrates your esteem for people outside your work area

497 To facilitate the associate's integration into the social fabric of the company, provide a "buddy" who can act as a mentor when you are not available, giving the associate company during breaks.

Later

498 Speak positively and enthusiastically (but realistically) about the organization and its people. Don't poison the associate's view of people or departments that are not on your "A" list by running them down. Allow new employees to form their own opinions.

499 Establish an open-door policy so the associate has easy access to you when needed.

500 Follow up regularly to see how new associates are doing. Praise their accomplishments to increase their confidence and sense of satisfaction at having joined the organization.

501 Treat new associates as a resource. Coming from a different background and work experience, they will bring a fresh perspective and different work strategies that may bring about an improvement in the way you do things. Be receptive to their input by showing your interest and, where possible, acting on their suggestions.

502 Schedule regular meetings after the orientation to ensure that the associate is adjusting well to their new environment. Get their opinion on the orientation process should there be opportunities to improve it.

503 Consider inviting a person's family or significant other for an orientation to demonstrate your interest in their links outside the organization.

How to...
Be a catalyst for innovation

Why not go out on a limb? Isn't that where the fruit is?

– FRANK SCULLY

Young children are *the most creative human beings because they are free from the artificial limitations we learn growing up. Most people have their creative spark drummed out of them by the time they've left school. However, the best solutions to difficult problems are usually the creative ones. Here's how to encourage innovative thinking and action among your associates:*

504 Seek out and attract creative people to your team. They

✓ may be unconventional (in their approach, dress, etc.)
✓ often appear to be troublemakers
✓ are persistent
✓ are willing to take risks
✓ have vivid imaginations

505 Encourage calculated risk-taking by rewarding efforts and process, as well as results. Doing so sends a clear message that the action is as important as the outcome.

506 Look for small improvements rather than expect major ones; base hits are important since they set the stage for home runs.

507 Set up an experimentation budget to show your interest in new initiatives.

508 Allow mistakes. It's impossible to make significant improvements without errors. Don't look at failure as the end of the road. Consider it a stepping-stone. Involve your people in finding out what went wrong and how obstacles can be overcome.

509 Support persistence. Not all innovations come from flashes of imagination. Sometimes real innovations come from hours, days, and even years of trial and error.

510 Be open and responsive to new ideas. Listen to be influenced rather than to rebut.

511 If you find it difficult to assess the merits of a new idea, find someone who can and who might advocate on behalf of the idea.

512 Maintain a relaxed atmosphere. Having fun creates a playful environment that encourages creativity.

513 Encourage foolish or impractical ideas, if they don't have an immediately negative influence on your business. These ideas can often lead to new innovations.

514 Challenge people to come up with new ideas daily.

515 Leave a flip chart in the work area. Encourage people to record ideas as they occur. Share and evaluate these with your people at your next meeting.

516 Go outside of your industry to look for new ideas that could work for you. While you may get ideas from similar work areas within your organization, you will find more innovative solutions by looking to other organizations and industries.

517 Challenge yourself and your staff to think of more reasons why a new idea would work than reasons it would not.

518 Harness the creativity and ingenuity lying dormant in your people. Involve them when you have a significant challenge. Do this by informing them of the problem and inviting their input. Give them time. The more you give your associates time to incubate, the more creativity results.

519 If you gather people together, give them a process that will encourage out-of-the-box thinking.

520 Include as many of the people who are affected by the problem as is practicable.

521 Select people with different skill sets. Creativity is best stimulated by a mix of people with different mind-sets, backgrounds, and perspectives. Choose people who are open to new ideas because rigidity tends to shut off new ideas prematurely. Include a maverick to act as a catalyst for ideas if the team requires an impetus to think creatively.

522 Meet in a new location if possible. Choose an unusual and informal place so the team can feel comfortable and open up.

523 Make sure you have a flip chart and Post-it™ Notes in the room to record all the ideas.

524 Start with an icebreaker to get people talking – this could be anything from finger food to a short experiential exercise that demonstrates the power of teamwork. Encourage an understanding and appreciation of each member's ability and the reason why each has been chosen.

525 If you are going to use Brainstorming as an idea-generating process, appoint one or more people to capture the ideas. Remind participants of the guidelines and post them where they can be seen and referred to. These rules typically include:

- ✓ the importance of quantity over quality
- ✓ no discussion until all ideas are recorded
- ✓ the avoidance of criticism
- ✓ recording of all ideas

526 Give time for ideas to be considered before generating them. This allows introverts time to think before they are overwhelmed by the ideas of the extreme extroverts.

527 Conduct a round robin: ask each person in sequence for one idea at a time. The key here is speed – to get as many ideas as possible. People who are out of ideas may pass.

528 Piggyback on ideas. This involves revisiting some of the more general ideas on the flip chart and using them as inspiration for new ones or variations on a theme. This is a good strategy when the group's ideas appear to have dried up.

529 Incubate ideas after a creative session is over. Give everyone time to mull over the ideas proposed. This is a good strategy when it appears that the meeting has lost momentum – you simply schedule another session and send people home to think about the ideas generated so far.

530 Evaluate all ideas. After the team has generated a list of ideas, they need to be pruned to those that are

- ✓ novel
- ✓ cost effective
- ✓ of benefit to as many stakeholders as possible
- ✓ easy to implement
- ✓ can be implemented quickly
- ✓ likely to attract the least resistance

How to...
Be a better listener

The older I grow, the more I listen
to people who don't say much.

– GERMAINE G. GLIDDEN

You cannot learn without listening, *and you cannot lead without learning. Many business disasters have come to pass simply because no one was listening when a serious problem was identified. On the positive side, listening will increase your influence, the confidence of your staff, and the reserve of information with which you can make informed decisions. Here are the guidelines for good listening:*

531 Pay attention. Give the other person your full attention. Set aside your work and do not take phone calls while you are listening.

532 Meet in a quiet place. Step away from the noise and distractions that may hinder your listening.

533 Focus on listening. Listen to be influenced without developing a rebuttal partway through the process. Don't allow your mind to leap ahead to arguments or conclusions. Simply take in the message you are being given.

534 Don't interrupt. Let people finish their thoughts and ideas.

Only stop a monologue when the same point is being rehashed again and again. Then, you may interrupt to indicate that you have heard and understood.

535 Let the person speak. Even when the other person is stumbling to make a point, don't interrupt or correct. Get in the habit of counting to five before you interject or respond.

536 Show your interest. You can do this by nodding, saying "yes," or changing your facial expressions to reflect the message you are taking in.

537 Be there. Maintain good eye contact. Don't stare, but give your full visual and mental attention to the other person.

538 Keep track of your body language. Your posture reflects your attitude. You can demonstrate an open, receptive approach by:
- ✓ leaning forward.
- ✓ looking interested.
- ✓ facing the other person.
- ✓ smiling or showing your reaction by facial expression.

539 Check your understanding. You want to be sure you understand what is being said. One way to do this is to ask, "So what you are saying is X. Is that right?" Allow the person to correct you if you have misunderstood.

540 Ask questions. Questions show your interest, allow you to check your understanding, and help you get at the feelings behind the facts.

541 Keep an eye on non-verbal reactions. People display their true feelings and opinions without uttering a word. Gestures, eye movements, posture, and facial expressions can tell you more than words.

542 Stay with the speaker. Don't leap to conclusions. Refrain from filling in the gaps. Stop yourself from formulating a response ahead of time.

543 Don't rush ahead. Don't finish other people's sentences.

544 Show empathy. Even if you disagree with what the other person is saying, they must have a reason for saying it. Try to understand that reason and their point of view.

545 Accept silence. Learn to accept brief, natural lulls in conversation. Silence encourages the other person to continue sharing.

How to...
Create a learning environment

Brains must replace physical goals and equipment as the main source of value.

– NOEL M. TISHEY

*M*ost organizations *have human resources departments. The concept of human resources suggests that employees are assets that need to be nurtured, grown, and developed. The reality is most often the opposite. When budgets are cut, training programs are usually the first to go, even though most executives acknowledge that knowledge is a key competitive weapon.*

Creating a learning organization – one in which employees are constantly developing their knowledge and expertise – is not a question of sending people to more workshops. On the contrary, formal learning is only a small part of the development equation. Here is a list of alternative strategies to develop knowledge.

546 Encourage continuous learning. Ensure that the primary focus of annual performance reviews is the future, not the past. Have your managers create learning plans for each individual that will promote continuous learning from a variety of sources.

547 Ensure that performance reviews are done regularly and that they always have learning plans.

548 Allow employees the flexibility to learn in the way that suits them best, be it by personal research, having a buddy help them, being coached by someone internal or external to the organization, participating in workshops (especially those that give them the opportunity to meet with peers from other organizations), joining professional associations, participating in webinars and/or attending conferences.

549 Maximize the value of any formal learning by requiring that employees debrief and teach others what they have learned while away from work.

550 Create self-directed learning teams. Encourage those employees for whom self-development is a high priority to form volunteer learning groups that meet regularly.

> ✓ These meetings should be self-directed, allowing the members to decide
>   - how often they will meet
>   - where they will meet
>   - what topics will be covered
>   - who will facilitate the learning of each topic
>   - the length of each meeting
>
> ✓ Learning teams are more successful when they are voluntary. This will promote enthusiasm, pride, and ownership.
>
> ✓ Include members from different work areas, promoting cross-pollination of ideas and breaking down barriers between work areas.
>
> ✓ Cover bite-sized topics, including managerial, organizational, and technical subjects of interest to all members.
>
> ✓ Allow time between meetings to give members the opportunity to apply their learning.

551 Regularly survey stakeholders – both customers and employees – to identify new opportunities to serve them better. Prioritize opportunities and implement changes.

Monitor improvements and ensure that employees who produced the improved performance are acknowledged.

552 Establish task forces to recommend new solutions to old problems. Include the employees needed to implement the solution. Have line employees take responsibility for implementing these ideas. Share new ideas with other parts of the organization so benefits can be maximized across the organization.

553 Use measurement to promote learning. Measure performance in each area of the organization as it relates to revenue/costs, client/customer satisfaction, and/or staff morale. Display charts of key performance indicators for all to see. Meet regularly with employees to review performance. If the indicators show an improvement, determine what has been done to bring this about so it can be repeated. If performance has declined, determine the root cause to prevent it from happening again. Share both good and bad data with all associates and encourage them to learn from both. Reward changes in behavior and practice as may be appropriate.

554 Celebrate innovative actions, even those that prove to be mistakes. That's right! Encourage people to try new ideas. But turn failures into positive experiences by analyzing what went wrong and how the mistake can be avoided next time. Needless to say, actions with the potential for major mistakes – such as those involving the health and safety of employees – should always be avoided.

555 Meet regularly with fellow managers, both inside and outside your organization, to establish best practices. Keep an open mind to new ideas, even when at first glance they don't seem to fit your circumstances. Share some of these new ideas with your employees and invite their feedback. Allow ideas to percolate until they are dismissed, used in part, or fully adopted.

556 Encourage your managers to learn from each other and to maximize the value of learning from whatever sources they use. Reward managers who share ideas openly.

557 Continuously benchmark key processes. Identify new performance targets and best practices by

- ✓ allowing your employees to define what they could best learn from other organizations
- ✓ identifying organizations that have similar processes but are in another industry (you're bound to find fresh ideas)
- ✓ allowing your employees, not a consultant, to do the data collection. This will increase enthusiasm for and commitment to implement the new ideas.

How to...
Present like a star!

*Speeches are like babies – easy
to conceive, hard to deliver.*

– Pat O'Malley

*A***nyone in management** *who wants to be taken seriously needs to be able to present their ideas with conviction. You can have the best ideas in the world, but if you can't sell them, they will die on the vine. Here's how to get ready for a presentation and how to conduct it with maximum impact.*

Preparation

558 Learn all you can about your audience. Discover their hot buttons.

559 Prepare your presentation. Assemble appropriate supporting documentation. If the presentation is complex, have a package of information prepared for each participant (distribute in advance if possible).

560 Decide on the best medium for your presentation. People require about forty percent less time to grasp a concept with visual aids than with verbal instruction alone. The most commonly used media today are computer-generated PowerPoint™ slides projected with an LCD projector. But, flip charts are very appropriate if not more desirable for an informal small-team presentation.

561 Remember, your audience will absorb information in three ways:

✓ visual
✓ auditory
✓ kinesthetic

Your presentation should include all three for maximum impact. Getting people involved is very often challenging, especially if the audience is large and time is limited.

562 Plan your agenda. For example, an agenda that requires approval for resources will cover

✓ welcome and introductions
✓ objectives and agenda
✓ the issue
✓ the recommendations
✓ the benefits
✓ your action plan
✓ questions and answers
✓ request for go ahead
✓ wrap up

563 In preparing your slides, it is best to

✓ Keep them short and to the point.

✓ Use one idea per slide.

✓ Add a picture where possible.

✓ Make sure letters are large, bold, and printed legibly in dark colors.

564 Plan your presentation to last no more than fifteen to twenty minutes. For simpler proposals, shorter is better. Use the KISS principle (keep it short and simple).

565 Assemble all your information and do a dry run beforehand. Imagine the audience in front of you. Gauge their reaction.

566 Assemble an emergency kit of markers, masking tape, name cards, spare bulbs, pencils, and pens.

567 Give people plenty of notice of your presentation. Confirm their attendance.

Set-up

568 Get to the meeting room early. Make sure the seating arrangement and equipment is as you requested.

569 Check all equipment. If you are using any electronic equipment make sure you know how it works and that it does work.

570 Ensure that you have an IT person available in case something goes wrong. The more important the presentation, the greater the chance something might go wrong – that's Murphy's Law.

571 Check the view from several seats to make sure everyone can see the screen.

572 Prepare places for each person, providing writing paper and pens if necessary. However, do not hand out your presentation in advance – people will tend to read your material instead of listening to you. Pass it out at the end of the presentation.

Conducting the Presentation

573 Relax, and welcome people into the meeting room. Show your confidence and approachability with a firm handshake and a smile.

574 When all are seated, welcome everyone officially and let them know what to expect. Remind them of your agenda, the expected outcome(s), the amount of time you intend to take, and any breaks. Let them know you will give them a copy of the presentation at completion. Also, let them know where the washrooms and fire exits are.

575 Let people know if you intend to take questions as they occur or whether you prefer them at the end of the presentation. The former approach will show greater interest in the attendees and demonstrate greater confidence in your ability.

576 Follow your agenda step-by-step.

577 Start off with as much impact as possible. Present a challenge or recount a story that will enable you to connect with the audience and grab their attention.

578 Ask rhetorical questions from time to time. Challenge your audience. Conduct periodic polls by asking a question that requires a show of hands.

579 When you conduct a question and answer session, focus on those people who are likely to be constructive and positive.

580 If a question comes from someone who rambles a lot, you might say, "Can you summarize your ideas in about twenty words?"

581 Paraphrase questions to give yourself time to formulate what answer you will give. It will also orient people who didn't hear the question the first time.

582 If hostile people attempt to destroy your presentation,

✓ do not become defensive
✓ do not engage in verbal sparring

- ✓ use humor to diffuse tension
- ✓ give facts rather than opinions
- ✓ canvass other opinions to show alternative approaches
- ✓ offer to deal with their issues
- ✓ offer to deal with their issues offline if they are unrelated to your topic

583 Keep the presentation short and to the point. Don't cover material that is already known to the audience. Focus on new information.

584 Do not read word-for-word from your notes, slides, or overheads. The audience can do that too. Give people a chance to read each visual, then paraphrase the content, stressing key points.

585 Provide a bridging comment between overheads and slides so your presentation is knitted together.

586 Maintain eye contact with your audience:

- ✓ Scan the audience, looking at each person for three to five seconds.
- ✓ Don't read off the screen or turn your back on the audience.

587 Keep people's attention by

- ✓ changing the pace of presentation from time to time
- ✓ doing something different at least every seven minutes (asking questions, polling the audience, completing questionnaires, doing group work, and so on)
- ✓ modulating your voice (speak loudly and then softly, quickly and then deliberately)
- ✓ animating your facial expressions and gestures
- ✓ punching the air on key points

588 Move around the room getting closer to your audience when they ask questions. Staying behind a podium will build a wall between you and your audience.

589 End on a high note. Confirm with the attendees that the objective has been met.

How to...
Be a problem solver, not a problem maker

Yesterday's answer has nothing to do with today's problem.

– BILL GATES

Inefficiency in most companies is caused by continually re-"solving" the same problem. Here are four simple hints to turn your team's problems into opportunities – or make them disappear for good.

590 Prioritize the issues

✓ Pick the most important issues first. Start with those causing the most customer complaints, greatest costs, and/or most conflict.

✓ Address problems in your own backyard before you go on the hunt for other people's problems.

✓ Tackle the problems you have control over before breaking your teeth on those beyond your control.

591 Break the problem down

✓ Disassemble a problem into its components and find solutions for each issue. Start with the largest first and continue systematically through the issues until you are done – or the remaining issues are too small and petty to warrant any further attention.

✓ Establish a process for solving problems. A good one is: Define the Issue Clearly, Find the Cause, Find Solutions, Plan, Implement, Monitor. Post this in a prominent place and encourage your team members to use it every time they're confronted with a problem. Always remember that solutions come after analysis of the causes, not before.

592 Get the facts

✓ Problems often result from missing information. Find the facts about each of your problem's components and you will probably find a solution much more easily.

✓ If the problem is well known and requires a quick solution, consider asking opinions of the people involved.

✓ Ensure that you have determined the root cause of the problem before you get to the solution.

✓ Understand your problem clearly by defining it in terms of the five Ws and an H: the What, Where, When, Who, Why, and How of the problem.

✓ Involve the people who will need to implement changes.

593 Find new innovative solutions to problems that keep coming back

✓ Aim for creative, original solutions to problems. Brainstorm with the entire team.

✓ Encourage wacky suggestions – they often contain the germ of the solution.

Part of my job is to keep a vague sense of unease through the entire company. The minute you say the job is done, you're dead.

– ARTHUR MARTINEZ

How to...
Manage projects on time and on budget

> *We cannot become what we want to be by remaining what we are.*
>
> *– MAX DEPREE*

*M*ost organizations *use project teams to manage significant change initiatives. They are a key process to spur improvement, especially when they are interdisciplinary, as most are. Project teams present project champions a chance to either shine or be tagged as incompetent. Although projects court disaster the way royalty attracts bad biographers, with a little luck and lots of good management, you can keep your project from being trashed.*

Here are some important tips to increase your probability of success significantly:

594 Don't start before you have a specific and detailed mandate from someone at a significant level in the organization.

595 Get a clear understanding of the expectations and deliverables. This will give you focus and reduce time wastage. Typical projects focus on research and recommend or implement change.

596 Establish the parameters of the project in terms of

- ✓ geography
- ✓ parts of the organization that may be impacted, including organizational levels
- ✓ your authority
- ✓ products or services
- ✓ systems and processes

597 Assemble the best team. In doing so, determine

- ✓ Does the team have adequate representation from areas likely to be affected?

- ✓ Do they have enough time, or will they make the time to participate fully?

- ✓ Is there a good distribution of relevant and helpful skill sets?

- ✓ Do the people involved have a good grasp of the fields covered by the project? As an obvious example, if part of the project is setting up a database, you will need, at the least, an expert in information architecture and one in the specific field from which the data will be drawn.

Is a variety of viewpoints and methodologies represented? Do the team and project have a sponsor?

598 Meet with your team and start off on the right foot.

- ✓ Welcome your team and explain the project mandate, its importance, the parameters, why they were chosen, and your overall plan. Get buy-in.

- ✓ Create ground rules that establish how the team will work together. These may include ideas such as
  - being open to new ideas
  - participating fully
  - completing assignments on time
  - helping each other when a member is overloaded
  - spreading the workload
  - informing the project manager if they are experiencing

a problem that may delay the project or cause it to go over budget

✓ Draw up some organizational guidelines such as when you will meet, how often, and where. These should grow naturally from the plan's goal breakdown. It is essential to get team buy-in to these structures.

✓ Quickly brainstorm to anticipate potential obstacles and roadblocks and incorporate ways to overcome them in the overall plan.

✓ End the meeting on a positive note by explaining how the project's success will benefit team members.

599 Develop a work plan. Working with the team, break the project down into measurable, quantifiable steps (goals), and make each step essential to the completion of the project.

✓ Use appropriate tracking tools to document your plan. There are many sophisticated yet simple software packages that will enable you to produce Gant charts or PERT (Program Evaluation and Review Technique) charts to guide and monitor your activities. Set specific deadlines for each step.

✓ Assign specific people to each goal.

✓ Determine the basic roadmap for reaching each goal.

✓ Get endorsement of your plan from the project sponsor.

600 Manage the process.

✓ Monitor progress through the achievement of the plan's subsidiary goals. Make a visual progress chart to encourage responsibility and boost morale.

✓ Supervise, don't substitute. Only if someone is not doing the work, replace them or call in additional resources and personnel. Your task is to manage your team, be a role model (stay out of office and departmental politics), focus on the big picture, link it to an overall vision, and run inclusive and concise meetings that follow specific agendas.

- ✓ Issue periodic progress reports to team members to boost morale and make them feel appreciated.

- ✓ Recognize individual excellence and transmit this commendation to the team and the member's boss.

- ✓ Modify the project plan and parameters as necessary.

601 Anticipate problems. Things will seldom go according to plan. You can give a problematic project a final push toward completion by

- ✓ increasing your effort input to output ratio by a factor of ten (doing ten times the work you think is necessary)

- ✓ bringing in the cavalry – a friend, mentor, or colleague who can support and advise you

- ✓ maintaining forward momentum – by moving forward every week, you will drag the rest of the project with you

- ✓ including focus groups of primary consumers and modifying project aims and parameters to create extraordinary outcomes based on their information

- ✓ keeping a reserve – try to allow for about twice as much time and expense as you think you will need

602 Wrap up on a high note if you have been successful.

- ✓ Present your project findings to senior management to get buy-in and recognition.

- ✓ Celebrate the conclusion in an appropriate way. A meal or gift vouchers are two ways to thank your team members.

Remember the old saying that "crisis is another name for opportunity."

How to...
Build a new team

> *Someone said that the membership of*
> *a club is made up of four kinds of bones.*
> *There are WISHBONES, who spend their time wishing*
> *someone else would do the work.*
> *There are JAWBONES, who do all the talking but little else.*
> *Next come the KNUCKLEBONES, who knock*
> *everything that everyone else tried to do.*
> *And finally, there are the BACKBONES,*
> *who get under the load and do the work.*
>
> *– ANONYMOUS*

Doing some planning before a team is constituted will help you choose members wisely and keep the team running successfully.

Designing the Team

603 Understand the purpose of the team. Be clear about

- ✓ who the stakeholders are
- ✓ what their expectations are
- ✓ what the team will be doing
- ✓ whether it will be temporary or permanent
- ✓ who your client/customers are
- ✓ how you will measure success
- ✓ what potential roadblocks exists

604 Determine the best structure for a new team. This will be influenced by its mandate, deliverables, and whether it is temporary or permanent. Decide whether the team should be cross-functional or a collection of people doing similar tasks. This decision will be influenced by whether your organization needs to break down interdepartmental barriers or create commitment to a common goal within the area.

Selecting Team Members

605 Recruit the most talented team of employees with complementary skills you can find. Be sure to pick people who also have a high level of emotional maturity so they are able to develop respectful relationships with each other.

606 Develop a profile sheet for each person and position on the team. Your description should include

- ✓ previous experience on a team
- ✓ previous work experience
- ✓ technical skills required
- ✓ communication
- ✓ willingness to take responsibility
- ✓ self-confidence
- ✓ relevant education

607 If you are just the sponsor, select the team leader. If possible, involve team members in the selection so they will choose someone who has credibility with them. An effective leader will be someone who

- ✓ is well organized
- ✓ knows how to delegate
- ✓ encourages participation
- ✓ listens
- ✓ understands the corporate culture
- ✓ is able to give constructive feedback
- ✓ understands team dynamics
- ✓ motivates

608 Select team members. While ten to twelve may be an ideal number, teams as small as five or as large as fifteen can work well too. Recruit people with complementary technical and social skills. There is strength in diversity. For example, having a devil's advocate will challenge the group to search for more alternatives before making decisions. This will enhance creativity and the quality of decisions.

Starting

609 Describe the purpose of the team and create a mission statement. Involve the team so they have a sense of ownership. Post the mission in a visible place and have everyone sign it.

610 Clarify roles, boundaries, and expectations. The clearer it is to team members how they will operate, the quicker they will get going and the fewer the conflicts. They also need to know how they fit into the overall framework and strategy.

611 Transfer increased responsibility to the team as fast as the associates are willing and able to take it. If the team is a permanent one, it should assume as much responsibility for its own management as possible. Develop a milestone chart to promote the orderly transfer of tasks to the team. Ensure a training plan is in place to make this happen

612 Gather the team together so you start on the right foot with everyone having the same clear expectations. Call a meeting. Be sure your agenda will

✓ explain the purpose of the team

✓ indicate what the goals are and how these will be measured

✓ establish the rewards for goal achievement

✓ share your strategy for improving performance with the team. If you don't have a strategy, ask for input. If you have one, ask for feedback.

✓ spell out the benefits of participating on the team. If members see what's in it for them, they will be enthused about other benefits

✓ negotiate the ground rules. Using a flip chart, identify key behaviors that will enable team members to work together in harmony. Confirm agreement to the rules. Post the ground rules in a prominent place to ensure that they are not forgotten

✓ identify skills of team members to see how they complement each other

613 Meet regularly, formally or informally, so momentum does not stop.

614 Celebrate successes, particularly measurable benchmarks. Celebrations increase cohesiveness and develop a sense of pride.

615 Allow team members to take on as much responsibility as they are willing to and are trained for. Increasing delegation of responsibility over time will increase ownership for performance among team members.

How to...
Get the monkey off your back (or increase responsibility and accountability)

Purposeful organizations are exciting, inspiring places to work. Purpose inspires even the most mundane task with meaning.

– Lorin Woolfe

*T*oo often we describe ideal leaders *as tough, decisive, and assertive. They're in charge – certainly a good model for getting things done in a hurry. Indeed, in urgent situations, this is the appropriate approach. But a different style would work better in situations where there's time to deal with complexity and when creativity and commitment are important!*

The collaborative approach has other, long-lasting benefits – it spreads responsibility to those who need to take ownership. Performance is unlikely to be at an acceptable level without that sense of ownership. To increase feelings of ownership, leaders need to do the following:

616 Be clear to the employees you work with how decisions will be made – which decisions are to be taken by one person or a few and which require more general acceptance and (ideally) a general consensus.

617 Identify and document (in job descriptions) the aspects of performance that each employee member is accountable for. Wherever possible, establish measurable indicators to track whether that person is performing according to expectations.

618 Define responsibilities at the end of every meeting. As decisions are being made, a secretary/recorder should note exactly what commitments have been made, who undertook to do what, and when it is to be done. "ASAP" or "soon" is not a commitment! It's a vague statement of intention that can easily slip between the cracks.

619 Give feedback when commitments are met – and especially when they are not. People need to know which obligations are taken seriously. As a leader, your attitude toward meeting obligations will send a clear message about what is important. If you are seen to accept ongoing non-fulfillment of obligations, you will breed a culture of laissez-faire performers. Letting people know about your disappointment when deadlines are missed is important too. Consider involving your team in deciding how to deal with "breaches of contract." Often a small fine, such as a dollar, for coming late to a meeting, is sufficient punishment for infractions. This highlights the transgression instead of accepting it as normal.

620 Display an action board in the workplace so everyone can see what outstanding tasks they have. Visibility will increase the chances of things getting done.

621 Be a role model. Live up to the expectations people have of you. Always meet your commitments and don't offer excuses when you can't. A simple apology and acknowledgment will suffice.

How to...
Conduct a formal training session

> *There are three kinds of business people:*
> *successful, unsuccessful, and those who give seminars*
> *telling the second group how the first group did it.*
>
> *– REY CARR*

*O*ne of the most important challenges *for leaders is to develop the talents of subordinates so others can perform at the highest level. Also, when you move on up the corporate ladder it is important that others have the ability to carry on effectively in your absence. There are many ways to train people, but one of the most effective is to conduct workshops for a few people at a time. If done properly, this is economical and effective.*

Planning the Session

622 Schedule your training near the time the skills need to be implemented. There is little point in training people too far in advance as retention will decline over time. Training after your associates have started the job will require some unlearning since they may have developed bad habits.

623 Ask yourself whether training will benefit your clients or customers. If not, it may be wasting the organization's time and money in a way that will add little value.

624 Determine whether people need knowledge, skills, or both. If skills are needed, you will need to incorporate practice into your workshop.

625 Plan short sessions. People retain skills more effectively if you divide training into half-day lesson modules.

626 Consider buying a packaged program if your development costs are high. Avoid packages that

- ✓ cannot be customized
- ✓ have audio-visuals from a very different industry
- ✓ are aimed at a very different audience level
- ✓ are made in a foreign country

627 Find out about your trainees. You should know

- ✓ what previous courses they have done
- ✓ what they need to know
- ✓ what they need to do better
- ✓ their motivation level
- ✓ their literacy level

628 Develop materials to suit the audience. For example, materials for people with poor literacy should have more pictures and diagrams. Materials will be better if they

- ✓ contain one idea per page
- ✓ are written in simple language
- ✓ have lots of space to make notes
- ✓ are interactive – have spaces for people to write answers, do quizzes, and complete checklists

629 Book meeting rooms early. Advise attendees of the location and give maps if necessary.

Before the Session

630 Get to the training room early. Check your equipment.

Arrange seating to suit the purpose of the session. Use

- ✓ theater style for a show and tell
- ✓ U-shape for interactive training
- ✓ round tables for teamwork exercises

Before Starting

631 Mingle with participants to establish rapport. Greet them warmly and show your enthusiasm for the session and their participation

At the Start of the Session

632 Begin on a high note. Memorize the opening to start off strongly and set the tone for the workshop. If you are not a senior executive, consider having a highly regarded executive kick off the session to stress the value of the workshop.

633 Develop a contract at the onset about what you expect of participants and what they can expect of you. Remind them that

- ✓ they are responsible for their own learning
- ✓ they should let you know if their needs are not being met
- ✓ you will be starting and finishing on time

Also, let people know

- ✓ the location of fire exits
- ✓ telephone availability
- ✓ washroom locations
- ✓ break times and length

634 Get everyone comfortable through some kind of icebreaker. Introduce yourself and get people to introduce themselves. If your audience is a little reluctant at first consider allowing them to interview the person sitting next to them and then sharing with the class their partner's

✓ name
✓ job and special skills
✓ key objectives
✓ concerns about the workshop

635 Make the objectives of the program clear. Post them in an area of high visibility.

636 Review the agenda so people know how you aim to achieve your objectives.

During the Session

637 Manage your time:

✓ Note restarting times on the flip chart.

✓ Don't wait for stragglers. Close the door at the agreed-on starting time

✓ Don't summarize for people who come in late.

638 If things don't go according to plan, don't raise awareness of the problem by apologizing.

639 Don't be afraid to admit you don't have an answer to a question. Ask the others if they have the answer. If not, offer to get back to the person. Don't lie or guess. Your integrity and honesty could be compromised and, with it, your ability to influence the audience.

640 Communicate at the audience's level. Avoid using complex words like "parameter" that send the message you are more theoretical than down-to-earth.

641 Use visuals to complement your verbal information wherever possible. They are six to eight times more effective than verbal instructions alone. If you use any diagrams, make sure they are culturally neutral.

642 Keep changing the pace to ensure that your audience has no time to get bored. Remember, the attention span of most adults is about seven minutes. So change the tempo and presentation medium, and intersperse team tasks with individual assignments. Also, stop from time to time to poll the audience. Ask, for example, "How many of you have tried this?" A poll provides a welcome change of pace and may give you useful information.

643 Draw information out of the group wherever possible. Their participation creates a change of pace and also validates your ideas in practical terms.

644 Avoid showing a video or conducting a lecture immediately after lunch since this is the time people have the least energy. Instead, schedule a fun activity or some physical exercise.

645 End your workshop with a challenge. Ask everyone to commit to using some part of the workshop in the next two weeks. Conduct a survey, one person at a time, of what their intentions are.

646 Ask people to write their action plans on a sheet of paper and place it in a self-addressed envelope. Mail these out sixty days after the workshop.

After the Session

647 Evaluate your training by whether participants put the skills to use, not by how much they enjoyed the program.

648 Set up refresher courses at which time you can confirm the effectiveness of the initial training, reinforce key skills, and add some new ones.

How to...
Deal with conflict between employees

If your neighbor does you some harm, do not pretend you are still friends ... do not hate him, but reprove him for what he did. Through this peace can be re-established.

– Rashbam

There is good conflict and bad conflict. Good conflict occurs when people challenge one another's ideas. It often leads to greater creativity. Poor conflict is where personalities come into play. This creates tension and distracts those involved from the task at hand. Others in your team may take sides in the dispute or be impacted by the negative atmosphere.

Conflict is stressful. It negatively impacts your working relationships and makes every task harder. Here are some ways you can address conflict:

649 When conflict occurs, assess the situation. Determine

✓ the size of the conflict. The bigger it is the more disruptive it may become and the greater the impact on other employees.

✓ the maturity level of the people involved. If they are mature and have a reasonable chance of resolving the issue themselves, then stay out of it and allow them to address it. Make them aware that you see there is a problem but that you are confident in their ability to deal with it.

650 If the issue is disruptive, impacting your team's morale, and has not been dealt with by the parties, get your head around the issue so you can intervene appropriately. If it is clearly the fault of one individual, deal with that person directly. If both share partial responsibility, get their agreement to intervene.

651 Set up a meeting. Make sure both agree to the meeting and come with open minds and are determined to address and resolve the issue. Make sure the meeting is not where others will see them and be speculating about the meeting's content. Also, make sure the combatants sit side-by-side, not across from one another. Have them facing a flip chart or whiteboard where the content will be displayed.

652 Set the tone for the meeting. Be assertive and empathetic throughout. Be sure not to take sides however tempted you may be.

653 Get agreement from both parties as to the desired outcome and the amount of time you expect to take. Book yourself off for twice the time. Establish, and get agreement to the objectives, time, process, and ground rules.

654 Have each person state their issues and interests. Record these on a flip chart or whiteboard and ensure that each associate has time to list all their items without interruption. When one is done, give the second associate the same opportunity.

655 Ask each person to restate the other person's issues and interests. This will demonstrate that they have listened to and understood the issues. If one associate has left out an important aspect that needs to be addressed, then prompt that individual to state their understanding of the issue.

656 Prioritize the issues. Ask both participants to identify the issues that upset them most.

657 Ask for solutions from the participants to address the issues raised. Record them to demonstrate that progress is being made. Develop a plan of action for each person that is specific and time based.

658 Summarize the meeting, acknowledging the difficulties that have been faced. Acknowledge the flexibility of each person as may be appropriate. Indicate that you will be following up to ensure that each person meets their commitments.

659 Follow up to check on progress. Acknowledge constructive behaviors. If commitments have not been met, deal with the individuals appropriately.

How to...
Handle conflict at meetings

> *Whenever you're in conflict with someone, there is one factor that can make the difference between damaging your relationship and deepening it. That factor is attitude.*
>
> – WILLIAM JAMES

*F*or a team to be truly effective, *it needs to meet from time to time to get updates, give feedback, make decisions, solve problems, and create plans. None of this can happen properly if there is tension and acrimony in the meeting room. Personality differences often come into play when people have different agendas, behave inappropriately, or dislike each other because of different approaches. In such circumstances it is vital that managers take action early to ensure that issues are dealt with before they become commonplace and pervasive.*

At Your Meeting

660 Create a climate for a good exchange of viewpoints. Be positive in your words and body language. Show that you are determined to resolve the conflict for the sake of everyone involved.

661 Make it clear that you know there are two sides to every story and that you may be part of the problem too.

662 State your case. Be clear and firm, but not accusing. Focus on the issue, not the person. For example, "I'm upset because the report was late" is better than "You didn't give me the report on time."

663 Be specific. Explain what is bothering you, but don't exaggerate. For example, say, "I'm disappointed the project was completed eight days late," rather than "You never get projects done on time" or "Your projects are always late."

664 Watch your temper. Inflammatory language only puts the focus on your anger, not on resolving the problems.

665 "Own" the problem. Use "I" statements instead of "you" statements whenever possible. For example, "I feel angry" is less likely to make a person feel defensive than "You make me angry."

666 Don't harp on old problems. Stick to the current agenda.

667 Listen fully to the other person's story. Don't interrupt. While you may disagree, look for points you can agree on. Nod or gesture to show your agreement.

668 Summarize what you heard to check your understanding. Show empathy. A statement such as "I would feel that way too" can go a long way toward easing anger and allows you both to get on with solving the problem.

669 Once the problem is understood on by both of you, and agreed move on to solutions. Offer ideas to address the other person's concerns. Ask for help in addressing your own concerns. Involving the other person in solutions increases the commitment toward resolution on both sides.

670 If a resolution cannot be reached, agree to disagree. Show your respect for the views of others, even if you don't agree with them.

671 Conclude the meeting with

- ✓ a brief summary of your discussion and the resulting solutions
- ✓ a statement of your appreciation for the other person's efforts to resolve your differences

After the Meeting

672 Keep in mind the issues raised at your meeting. Stick to your commitments. Show your appreciation when others do the same.

How to...
Make a speech that will knock people's socks off

> *One thing a speaker should remember for sure;*
> *the mind can absorb only what the seat can endure.*
>
> *– ANONYMOUS*

Making a speech is a difficult and intimidating task. But, as you move up the corporate ladder, you will need to make more and more speeches, both formal and impromptu. To a great extent, you will be judged not so much by what you say but by how you say it. Making a great speech isn't something you can learn through study. It takes time and practice. So, take every opportunity to speak in front of others until it becomes second nature and you're able to wing it with aplomb under almost any circumstances.

Here are some tips to make the process a lot easier.

Preparation

673 Accept only invitations with adequate lead times. If you don't have time to prepare and rehearse, decline.

674 Learn as much as you can about your audience. Find out about their

✓ age

✓ sex
✓ background
✓ education

675 Establish an objective and something you will say at the end to make the speech memorable. Work backward to craft your speech.

676 Draw a mental map of what you want to get across to your audience. Consider highlights and key points that will connect with your audience.

677 Order your key points so there is a natural flow of ideas.

678 Establish sub-points under each key item.

✓ Based on your confidence and memory, you can create a list of points you want to cover or more detailed notes to guide you. Don't write your speech out word for word. Reading it will bore your audience and cause you to speak in a monotone, increasing your discomfort since this is not your usual manner of speaking. If you are reasonably confident, consider recording your information on index cards as reminders or prompts. Use one card per key point.

679 Practice until you are confident. Your dry run can be done

✓ in front of a mirror
✓ into a tape recorder
✓ in front of a mentor
✓ on video

680 Avoid body language that projects insincerity, nervousness, or discomfort. Learn from the masters. Watch TV programs in which interviewees are drilled by experienced investigative reporters. Look for negative mannerisms to avoid.

681 Establish some good closing remarks that will summarize your key thoughts and leave the audience uplifted.

682 Visualize yourself making the speech with confidence. Imagining your success will increase the probability of it becoming reality.

683 Remember the three secrets of high impact presentations:

✓ Be sincere.

✓ Be quick.

✓ Be seated!

The Speech

684 Dress for the occasion. If you are unsure about the audience, dress up rather than too casually. Dress conservatively for most business situations.

685 Get to the meeting room early to familiarize yourself with the room and surroundings. Make sure all equipment (such as a neck-mic, projector, etc.) is working.

686 Tell people what you are going to tell them, tell them, and then tell them what you told them.

687 Grab the attention of your audience: Challenge them by starting off with one of the five Ws and an H:

✓ Who would like . . .?

✓ What would be the one . . .?

✓ When was the last time you . . .?

✓ Where is the best place you . . .?

✓ Why is it that . . .?

✓ How can you . . .?

688 Quote an alarming statistic or take a controversial stance.

689 Inject your remarks with humor, but only if you are good at telling jokes and only if the story is relevant to the subject. Avoid jokes that could offend. The best humor is a story that is self-deprecating. Not only will such a story amuse your audience, it will also help you connect with them since it demonstrates humility.

690 Project positive body language. A positive body posture will project confidence and make you feel good.

- ✓ Stand erect and tall.

- ✓ Push your chest out.

- ✓ Avoid putting your hands on one or both hips. Hands on both hips will separate your from the audience since it projects arrogance. A protrusion of one hip signals that you don't want to be there.

- ✓ Maintain steady eye contact with your audience. Fast-shifting eyes indicate a lack of certainty.

691 Use your arms to add impact.

- ✓ Open your arms to the audience, when appropriate, as if to embrace them. But, keep your arms at your sides when you are not using them.

- ✓ Keep arm gestures between your waist and shoulder.

692 Add impact with gestures. But avoid quick and jerky gestures and continuous single gestures since these give the impression of nervousness. Use gestures to suit your message, but don't overuse them or they will lose impact.

693 Use as much of the space in front of your audience as possible. Avoid standing behind a lectern, as it will distance you from the audience and make connection that much more difficult.

694 Use simple language to maximize the message. Words with more than two syllables are more difficult to understand. And, never use sexist language or say anything that would belittle any ethnic or minority group. You will offend your audience.

695 Create interest by involving your audience and changing your pace. For instance, take a poll, or ask for opinions. Find out if anyone can relate to the example you have described. This interaction will show you are interested in, and care for, the opinion of your audience.

696 Avoid going over material that is common knowledge. If you want to hold their attention, your information should be news to the audience.

697 Keep your audience's attention and make your speech interesting

✓ Illustrate points with anecdotes and quotes.

✓ Use props to add impact. Hold up articles, books, or magazines when you quote from recognized experts.

698 Change your voice modulation. Speak quickly, slowly, loudly, or softly for brief moments.

699 Pause before or after a key thought.

700 Make sure your end is as challenging as your introduction. Leave the audience with something to think about.

701 Avoiding nervousness: The biggest fear of North Americans, greater even than fear of death or snakes, is speaking to a group. Many a speech has been destroyed by anxiety. Here's what you can do to reduce your stress.

✓ Prepare thoroughly to improve confidence.

✓ Have cue cards or notes handy to reference if needed. But use them sparingly. Don't be tempted to read to the audience rather than conversing normally.

✓ Be yourself. Emulating someone else will make you feel awkward, and the audience won't buy it.

✓ Spend a few minutes alone before the presentation to collect your thoughts and focus your energy.

✓ Before you start, take a few deep breaths.

✓ Never admit you are nervous. Doing so will draw attention to the problem instead of your message.

✓ Maintain eye contact with a friendly face in the audience. Your confidence will increase. Similarly, avoid eye contact with someone who looks unhappy.

✓ Don't play with a pointer, pen, change in your pocket, your cue cards, or anything else that may be handy. You will distract the audience. Empty your pockets before your speech.

✓ If you have a small audience, begin your presentation casually with a two-way discussion of something topical. This will reduce tension and allow you to ease into your speech.

✓ Visualize your audience in a non-threatening way, such as in their underwear!

How to...
Facilitate teams in problem solving, decision making, and planning

> *It isn't where we came from;*
> *it's where we're going that counts.*
>
> – ELLA FITZGERALD

We all solve problems in our own particular way. While team problem solving can be very positive, it can be a real challenge to produce novel, innovative solutions with significant buy-in in a diverse work group. Here's how to get the benefits of teamwork without the traditional problems normally associated with team problem solving.

702 Identify a problem that lends itself to team problem solving. These tend to be problems that are

✓ complex
✓ require significant thought and study

703 Problems or opportunities are all around us. The most typical places to discover them include:

✓ customer feedback/complaints
✓ employee opinion surveys

✓ personal observations
✓ deviation from key performance goals

704 Assemble a team to deal with the opportunity. Choose team members who

✓ are affected by the problem
✓ have a stake in implementing a solution
✓ have an ability to think outside the box
✓ will make time to work on the issue
✓ care about the issue
✓ are able to work effectively in a team

705 Hold regular meetings to follow progress. These can be in person, by phone, or via the Internet.

706 At your first meeting, get agreement on how the team aims to be successful. Set ground rules for team meetings. These could include having a rotating chair, committing to start meetings on time, getting tasks delegated on time so as not to delay the project, and so on. Make sure these rules are accepted by the team, written down, and posted on the wall if necessary.

707 Set operational guidelines. They could include:

✓ how often you will meet, where, and when
✓ how you'll communicate between meetings
✓ how you'll deal with unrealistic or missed deadlines
✓ who is best able to handle certain tasks and how they'll be done

708 Get agreement to the answers to all of these questions and write the resolutions down.

709 Define the problem. Ask Who, What, When, Where, Why, and How (five Ws and the H) to define the problem clearly. For example, if the problem is "an atmosphere of antagonism," try to narrow it down more specifically, for example, "an atmosphere of antagonism exists between the marketing team and production team involved in Project X."

710 Establish the root cause of the problem. This can be done by

✓ seeking the opinions of people who are familiar with the issues

✓ analyzing any relevant data pointing to key issues

Again, use the five Ws and the H to ensure that causes are clearly established.

711 Find a solution. Brainstorm for all possible solutions by listing them without criticism or discussion. Ensure that everyone's opinion has been heard. Once ideas are generated, start a round of combining, removing duplication, clarification, and building on ideas (piggybacking).

712 Craft the most likely (cost-effective, time-effective, and personnel-effective) solution(s) into an action plan with specifically defined roles for each team member. Make sure the plan includes a concrete way to measure the success (or failure) of the plan, and specifically defined objectives.

713 Implement the plan. Follow up and monitor that the plan is being executed. Recognize new behaviors and extra effort.

714 Evaluate and monitor the outcome.

✓ Use the specific indicators embedded in the action plan to measure the success of the solution at the next team meeting (the meetings should continue until the problem is seen to have been resolved).

✓ Assess the benefits and costs of the solution to the area of the company affected by the problem and its solution.

✓ Evaluate the efficacy of your solution.

✓ Document your solution and its benefits, and post this on the department notice board as a template for other problem-solving teams to follow.

715 Recognize the team by celebrating appropriately.

As opera star Beverley Sills put it, "You may be disappointed if you fail, but you are doomed if you don't try."

How to...
DEAL WITH
EMPLOYEE
CHALLENGES

Lessons 716–794

How to...
Reduce absenteeism

Eating is not merely a material pleasure.
Eating well gives a spectacular joy to life and contributes
immensely to goodwill and happy companionship.
It is of great importance to the morale.

– ELSA SCHIAPARELLI

*A*bsenteeism costs everyone. *It increases your costs by necessitating the hiring of temporary staff and increased overtime. It reduces your customer service since fill-in staff is less effective. And it aggravates fellow employees who are often called upon to pick up the slack.*

You cannot avoid some absenteeism. But levels higher than ten percent indicate a serious problem. Levels below five percent are good. If you have a problem, here's how you can turn it around:

716 Keep statistics to pinpoint problems and trends. Your data log should tell you

- ✓ who was absent
- ✓ when they were absent
- ✓ why they were absent

717 Identify the size of the problem. Compare your data to other similar work areas. Find out if your employees' rate of absenteeism is

✓ better than average
✓ average
✓ worse than average

718 Analyze your data. Look for applications of the eighty/ twenty principle. You may find that

✓ twenty percent of your people are absent eighty percent of the time
✓ eighty percent of the absenteeism occurs on twenty percent of the days
✓ twenty percent of the causes account for eighty percent of the time off

719 Let your people know you are aware of, and concerned about, the problem. Ask for their help in dealing with the issue.

720 See if you can make improvements. Make sure your solutions relate to root causes, otherwise you'll simply be putting band-aids on the problem. Deal first with the problems you and your employees have control over. Typical causes of high absenteeism that you can improve include:

✓ boredom
✓ monotony
✓ poor supervisory practices including
  • lack of reward and recognition
  • lack of challenge
  • lack of responsibility
  • lack of feedback
  • low level of trust

733 Items you have little or no control over include

✓ personal problems
✓ sickness
✓ family problems (sick child, bereavement)

722 Deal with absenteeism immediately, whether your associate has been away for one day or one month. Discuss the issue with whoever was absent on their return to find out why they were away. Show your interest and/or concern.

723 Let new associate(s) know your attitude and the company's policies and procedures toward absenteeism during orientation. While your approach should not be threatening, people should know that consequences could include

✓ loss of pay
✓ hostility of peers who have to fill in or do extra work
✓ a note in their personnel record
✓ demotion
✓ termination

724 Be consistent, and follow company guidelines, but show empathy for those who are having a legitimate temporary problem. Work with them to get back on track.

Focus your energy on the minority of employees who are responsible for the most absenteeism.

How to...
Maintain a healthy and safe environment

Better a thousand times careful than once dead.

– PROVERB

*T**he health and safety of your staff** is as important as the happiness of your customer. As a manager, you have a legal and moral responsibility to ensure that the workplace is safe and that your staff's health is not in jeopardy. Here are some ideas for keeping the workplace safe:*

725 Make health and safety a top priority. Let your people know how you feel about the subject and what your mutual obligations are.

726 Deal with unsafe practices immediately. Make no exceptions. Allowing them to continue simply sets a dangerous precedent.

727 Share responsibility for health and safety with your team. Appoint a coordinator who can ensure that peers maintain safe practices. This person may serve on the health and safety committee.

728 Involve employees in finding ways to improve. This will demonstrate your faith in them and build ownership for new practices.

729 Find new and better ways of ensuring safety, even if you have the best record around. Keep yourself knowledgeable about current legislation as it relates to your role and responsibilities.

730 Always assume that what can happen will happen. Be proactive. Anticipate possible accidents and prioritize them in terms of probability and severity. Establish guidelines for dealing with accidents. Hold drills periodically to make sure people are able to respond appropriately at a moment's notice.

731 Post health and safety rules in a prominent place. Keep information up-to-date.

732 Spread ownership for health and safety issues by getting your employees to research and present a short topic at each meeting. Your encouragement plus a prize for the best presentation may act as an incentive.

733 Meet regularly with your people to review statistics and procedures. Celebrate improvements. Identify and remove causes of any decline in your performance.

734 Beware of fatigue caused by excessive work demands. Fatigue reduces concentration and makes people more vulnerable to accidents. They can fall asleep or make mistakes that might result in a serious accident.

735 Train people how to use machinery and equipment properly and safely. If hazards are high, training needs to be thorough. Procedures should be documented and properly enforced.

736 Keep the environment as safe as possible, and maintain good housekeeping practices. Repair damaged flooring, improve inadequate lighting, and replace poorly constructed furniture.

737 Review near accidents. They are danger signals.

738 Report and record all accidents, no matter how small. These statistics will help you analyze trends, pinpoint problems, and confirm the results of corrective actions.

739 Always have an adequate number of people on staff with current first-aid certification.

740 Make sure people use appropriate safety protection, but remember that protective gear is a last defense against injury, not a replacement for safety. Always stop work when conditions are hazardous.

741 Encourage a team approach. Reward and recognize people for taking care of one another.

742 Don't let new employees start work until they are fully briefed on your health and safety rules. Make them sign to confirm that they both understand the rules and undertake to abide by them.

How to...
Deal with abusive behavior

The greater the power, the more dangerous the abuse.

– EDMUND BURKE

***T**he obligations of leadership* in an organization go far beyond ensuring a profitable outcome. Indeed, the process of getting there is as important as the end result, for if the process is flawed, so too will be the final outcome.

Abusive managers and employees are a cancer that needs to be dealt with quickly, assertively, and professionally. Abusive people, left to their own devices, can wreak havoc in an organization. Unfortunately, they are not easily rehabilitated. They enjoy success and take all the credit while looking to blame others when performance has not met expectations. In positions of power, they maintain command and control by intimidation.

743 If you identify more than one individual who has a tendency to be abusive, consider your organization's culture:

✓ Is this behavior tolerated?

✓ Do you have a tendency to hire people who appear tough?

✓ Do you have such low opinions of employees that you see the need to have a task master?

744 Some organizations tolerate or even encourage abusive behavior, seeing it as a get-tough strategy to raise performance.

And, indeed, sometimes this approach works temporarily, but the change is likely to be short-term.

745 Consider the costs of inappropriate behavior. The cost to the organization is likely to be high and will include

- ✓ low employee morale, which in turn will result in lower productivity
- ✓ limited employee input in difficult situations, resulting in poor decisions and low levels of commitment
- ✓ hidden mistakes, with the resulting "blame game" destroying employees' self-esteem and confidence
- ✓ high employee turnover, leading to expensive recruiting, training, and disruption to customer service
- ✓ higher levels of sick leave and stress leave
- ✓ lawsuits against the company for harassment
- ✓ low levels of creativity and innovation (no matter how smart employees are, they will be unlikely to challenge the status quo as defined by their abuser)

If You Feel Your Behavior is Abusive

746 Confirm your observation. Get objective feedback on your performance. Undertake a 360-degree evaluation of your impact in the organization by enlisting a sample of at least five people who are likely to tell you how things really are rather than what you may want to hear. Expect no mercy, as the process is confidential. Then have a professional give you feedback so you can evaluate your strengths and weaknesses.

747 Create a plan that will enable you to slowly and systematically change the way you interact with others.

748 Get help. Find a professional who will be honest with you and can work you through the issues to change your behavior. An appropriate professional will be someone with a counseling background who is capable of winning your confidence, diagnosing the issues, and working with you on behavioral changes.

749 Meet with your key people and acknowledge the problem. This is a major step forward that will win you kudos for being courageous and humble. It will set a tone for others who may have similar or related issues. It will likely be the hardest thing you have ever done in your life. Tell your associates

✓ why you have taken the steps you have
✓ what you've discovered about yourself
✓ what actions you intend to take to make improvements
✓ you need their help in making the situation better. Invite them to give you feedback on your progress.

750 Take some courses that will help you become a better listener, be more humble, and become more skilled in empowering others.

751 Monitor your progress by observing the things you do and the reaction from others, as well as from the feedback you solicit from your employees and your coach.

752 Reward yourself by celebrating positive changes. Treat yourself to little luxuries that will reinforce the efforts you have made.

If Your Boss is Abusive

753 Be realistic about your chances of changing them.

754 Assess whether your manager is there for the short or the long term. If it's the former, you may want to wait it out in the hope that they will be fired or leave sooner rather than later. Their past record of employment may give you a clue how long they are likely to stay.

755 Consider looking for another job. If you feel the abuser will stick around and has the support of influential people – for example, on the board – then you need to be realistic. Either look for opportunities outside the organization, or try to find a way of working around that person.

756 If you are confident and assertive, push back appropriately. Let your boss know when their behavior is unacceptable. Be specific, calm, and respectful in your feedback. Ask for a change in approach, and explain how difficult it is for you to perform at the level expected when you are treated poorly.

If You Have an Abuser Reporting to You

757 Meet with the abuser to confront them about the issue. Be well prepared, since you can expect a hostile response and denial. Be frank, pointing out specific examples from what you have observed. Let them know the consequences of their behavior to the organization. Appeal to their commitment to the organization to correct the situation. If they refuse to acknowledge the problem, point out the serious consequences that lack of change will have on their career and the steps that will likely result.

758 Take the person out of a managerial role into an advisory, consultative, or technical role. The more power you can strip them of, the better.

759 Meet with the team who reported to the abuser. Deal with the topic professionally. Do not dwell on personalities, although you should acknowledge the problems. Ask the group for suggestions as to how the situation can best be turned around.

760 Before taking drastic action, consult with human resources to review the case and evaluate your options.

How to...
Deal with chemical abuse in the workplace

Drunkenness is the ruin of reason.
It is premature old age. It is temporary death.

– St. Basil

Abuse of drugs and alcohol in the workplace is a monumental problem. The costs in terms of lost productivity, higher absenteeism, and poor morale are just the tip of the iceberg.

And anyone can be an addict, from your CEO to your front-line worker. Here are practical ideas about what you can do:

761 Communicate regularly with your people. Be aware of the following symptoms of abuse:

- ✓ excessive absenteeism, particularly on Mondays
- ✓ regular tardiness
- ✓ declining productivity
- ✓ increased injuries and accidents
- ✓ personal problems – legal, financial, or family
- ✓ constant and/or suspicious phone calls
- ✓ physical deterioration such as slurred speech, runny nose, itchiness, and dry skin
- ✓ changes in interactions with others
- ✓ increased isolation from or conflict with peers
- ✓ rebellious behavior toward authority

✓ erratic behavior, mood swings, disorientation
✓ increased washroom visits

762 When you think there's a problem, you should

✓ prepare to deal with it assertively
✓ document signs and obvious patterns

763 Never allow the problem to fester once it has been detected. Don't

✓ enable the person to get away with poor job performance
✓ ignore or excuse unacceptable behavior
✓ take on the person's responsibilities
✓ make excuses to others, cover up the problem, pick up the slack, or fill in for them
✓ feel responsible
✓ solve problems you are not qualified to solve

764 Once the problem has been identified, confront the person with your evidence. This should be done privately and in a supportive manner. In your discussion you should

✓ avoid blaming, guilt tactics, or getting sidetracked with the associate's personal problems. Stick to work issues

✓ refer the associate to a professional to deal with personal problems. An Employee Assistance Program is geared to deal with these issues

✓ clarify goals and standards. The person should refocus on what is expected of them

✓ let the person know the consequences of poor performance

765 If performance does not improve, follow disciplinary steps according to company policy.

If you are unionized, involve your union representative to enlist their support in your actions, be they disciplinary or focused on rehabilitation.

How to...
Deal with harassment in the workplace

The first step in the evolution of ethics is a sense of solidarity with other human beings.

– ALBERT SCHWEITZER

*H*arassment is behavior that is unwelcome. *Harassment can take many forms and can be based on many things, including, but not limited to ethnic or national origin, sex, sexual orientation, marital status, age, or creed. Contrary to common belief, unreported harassment can and does exist, and it does not go away by itself. People in positions of authority, including managers and union representatives, are held legally accountable if they fail to act in an appropriately swift and decisive manner to counter workplace harassment. So what can you do?*

766 First, familiarize yourself with general company policy on harassment. Post that policy in a visible place in your department and give copies of it to your associates.

767 If your company has an educational video on forms of harassment, encourage your team to watch it during business hours.

768 Have on hand pamphlets or literature dealing with harassment.

Do not worry that you are giving your employees tools to use against you – you are empowering them.

769 Be a model of inclusionary, non-racist, non-sexist behavior. Use gender-neutral and race-neutral language. Indicate that there is zero tolerance for harassment in your department.

If Someone Comes to You with a Complaint of Harassment

770 Deal with the complaint right away to show you regard the alleged behavior as unacceptable.

771 Collect the facts swiftly, assertively, and with minimum disruption. Find out
- ✓ who the alleged harasser is
- ✓ what happened
- ✓ when and where it happened
- ✓ how often and for how long it has been happening
- ✓ whether they are aware the behavior was unwelcome
- ✓ whether there are witnesses
- ✓ what corroborative evidence exists

772 Determine the severity of the offence. In the case of sexual harassment, if the accused can be proved to have based a decision to hire on receiving sexual favors, or if the complainant was implicitly or explicitly threatened with job loss if sexual favors were withheld, severe punishment (dismissal) is appropriate.

773 Any form of harassment merits penalty if the harassment creates a hostile, offensive, or threatening work environment. Be cautious about determining the severity of the offence – if necessary, consult with your superior in the matter but do not involve anyone else.

774 Ensure there is no backlash against the complainant, and keep the complainant's confidentiality whenever possible.

If You Are Harassed

775 Confront the harasser and make your feelings known. If an apology is immediately forthcoming and the situation no longer recurs, you can choose to let it slide.

776 If the situation recurs or worsens, inform someone in authority immediately and assertively.

How to...
Create an innovative and creative culture

> *Behold the turtle! He only makes progress when he sticks his neck out.*
>
> *– ANONYMOUS*

The future of your organization will, in large measure, be determined by your ability to innovate and change so the value you're providing to stakeholders will be constantly increasing. The creative process, if properly employed, will allow you to move ahead – hopefully in quantum leaps. Here are some strategies you can use to become more creative. Encourage those around you to use them too.

For Yourself

777 Always be on the lookout for new ideas. Search the Internet, read books and magazines, and attend exhibitions and workshops.

778 Keep your mind open to ideas from unexpected places. Allow your mind to wander, especially in places you do not normally visit. Keep a pen and pad to jot down new ideas.

779 If you work with critical people, keep your ideas to yourself until you have had a chance to formulate them fully. With each idea, think about the benefits, drawbacks, and costs. Anticipate and find solutions to possible objections.

780 Don't exclude any ideas by determining in advance that others will not accept them. Don't concern yourself with selling the idea; that will be your last step. If you try to sell it before you're ready, you may inhibit your imagination and creativity.

781 Don't always expect to get home runs. Look for small improvements rather than major breakthroughs. Don't put undue pressure on yourself. As you become more innovative, your confidence will grow and so will the size of your ideas.

782 Secure a budget for some level of experimentation, including time and materials. This will send a strong signal to you and your colleagues about the importance the company places on innovation.

783 Allow for mistakes. Consider them stepping-stones on the way to success.

784 Be persistent. Sometimes skeptics will jump in quickly, especially if they know you are easily discouraged. If you are convinced your idea has merit, stick with it.

For Your Team

785 If you are open and responsive to new ideas from others, they will become more supportive of yours. Listen to be influenced rather than concentrating on developing a rebuttal.

786 If you find it difficult to assess the merits of your idea, find someone who understands it and who may become a spokesperson. Some people have more talent than others for being persuasive. Often it's not what you say but how you say it.

787 Make the tools of creativity freely available. A flip chart in your work area can be a place to post new ideas as they occur to people. People can also use Post-it Notes™ to jot down their ideas and leave them on the flip chart on their way past.

788 Look outside of your department or organization for new ideas that could work for you. While you may get ideas from similar work areas within your organization, you will find more innovative solutions in other organizations and industries. These ideas can be found by

- ✓ reading trade journals
- ✓ interviewing new employees who have worked for an organization that may have similar work processes
- ✓ attending conferences and shows where you can network with people from other organizations
- ✓ getting information from your trade organization
- ✓ scouring the Internet for ideas
- ✓ using the Internet chat features for sharing and researching new ideas

789 At your departmental meetings, take a leadership role by challenging your colleagues to think of more reasons a new idea would work, rather than reasons it would not.

790 At your performance reviews, comment on the employee's willingness and ability to welcome, find, and incorporate new practices and procedures into their daily work.

791 At each departmental meeting, review your operating statistics. If the numbers have improved, determine what might have been done differently. Incorporate these new practices into your everyday procedures. If your performance has declined, find out why and challenge your employees to identify new ways to improve.

792 Conduct regular brainstorming sessions to get people thinking about new possibilities. Give employees fair notice before a brainstorming meeting to allow them to come prepared with a list of their own. At each session, have one or two flip charts available to record all ideas. Then generate as many ideas as possible after explaining the rules of brainstorming to your team. They are

✓ the more ideas, the better

✓ no discussion until all ideas are recorded

✓ no idea is a bad idea

✓ no criticism is allowed

✓ all ideas are recorded

✓ building on ideas is encouraged (piggybacking)

793 There are two ways to collect ideas: The popcorn approach (where ideas can be generated by anyone), and a round robin (at which people are asked in sequence to give one idea at a time). People who don't have an idea can simply say "pass."

794 Another approach to creativity is the SCAMPER approach. Again, this is best done with the team. The essence of the approach is

✓ *Substitute*. Think of ways of replacing one thing for another. For example, could plastic replace wood, aluminum, or steel? Could electronic transfer replace the mail? Could a phone call replace a fax message?

✓ *Combine*. Are there ways of bringing things together that could result in one unique item? For example, could some services be combined to produce one-stop shopping?

✓ *Adjust, Add, or Adapt*. Figure out what changes can be made to improve products. Similar products could be added together, for example, such as two blades joined to create a twin razor. Adding stamps to one other can create a single roll or sheet. An alternative is to unite dissimilar products to create something new, such as a Swiss army knife.

✓ *Modify, Magnify, or Miniaturize.* Think about the possibilities of changing the size or the nature of the product itself. For example, Post-it™ Notes have done an exceptional job of taking the basic technology of a multiple-stick product to produce different sizes, colors, shapes, and uses.

✓ *Put Products to other uses.* This is a commonly used strategy. Excess newspapers can be made into fire logs; a kitchen knife can be used as a screwdriver.

✓ *Eliminate or Elaborate.* Consider the benefits that can be derived from less use. For example, packaging is reduced if refills are used. Generic products save on advertising.

✓ *Rearrange or Reverse.* Investigate the advantages of changing the order or sequence of events, or see if things can work the opposite way. One example with a twist on this theme would be a car that goes in two directions, not only one.

As Margaret Wheatley has said, "Only by venturing out into the unknown do we enable new ideas and new results to take shape."

VII

How to...
LEAD
STRATEGICALLY

Lessons 795–897

How to...
Recruit top talent

People are definitely a company's greatest asset. It doesn't make any difference whether the product is cars or cosmetics. A company is only as good as the people it keeps.

– MARY KAY ASH

With Baby Boomers leaving the workforce in droves over the next decades, smart organizations are gearing to fill the many gaps by identifying and developing their future leader and at the same time recruiting potential winners

Here are some ideas that will increase your probability of picking and retaining winners:

795 Constantly be on the lookout for exciting talent that will enhance your management bench strength. Keep all good résumés in a special file that can be accessed quickly.

796 Hire exceptional people even if you may not have an immediate opening for them. Put them to work on projects, research, or shadowing your best leaders so they can be parachuted into key positions that open up from time to time. In this way, they'll be able to hit the ground running and will have less need to establish their credentials with employees.

797 Give a bonus to employees for recommending great talent that ends up being hired. This is a lot more cost effective than using outside recruiters.

798 Treat your existing employees as the best source for promotions. It builds morale, especially among younger employees, when opportunities for promotion come up regularly.

799 Establish a rigorous process for recruitment, because mistakes can be very costly. Avoid the temptation to make decisions based on gut feeling.

800 An effective recruitment process should comprise numerous hurdles, including completion of an application, interviews, background checks, reference checks, ability and psychological tests, and, where possible, participation in an assessment center process.

801 Make sure you have a list of well-defined core competencies and the specific behaviors that are associated with each. This will enable interviewers to ask pointed questions that will give clues regarding the interviewee's ability in that area.

802 See to it that those who are doing the interviewing are properly trained. They should be familiar with the job description of the job to be filled and the company's core competencies, and have the ability to ask behavioral questions to confirm that the candidate can go beyond generalities and give specific examples of their actions that demonstrate ability in the specific area.

803 Use a team approach. People who are more senior should be interviewed by a number of people. Each participant in the process should rate the candidate numerically on a variety of criteria, the total of which should identify one candidate as being the most suitable. This should produce a consensus. Conduct a thorough background check to ensure that the résumé and interviews bear a close relationship to the individual's actual accomplishments

How to...
Use benchmarking to raise your performance bar

The best measure of one's talents is often how your peers grade your work.

– *AUTOMOTIVE INDUSTRIES MAGAZINE*

*E*very business, no matter what its size, *requires continual self-assessment and self-improvement to stay ahead of the game or, quite frequently, just stay in the game. This process of evaluation is known as benchmarking. It consists of five steps performed in an ongoing cycle designed to measure which processes perform adequately and which need to be improved.*

Benchmarking measures an organization's success or failure in specific areas by comparing them with other organizations that are known to perform that task very well. By looking outside the organization, managers will get a sense of what is possible and find new best practices that can be used.

There are two types of useful benchmarking. The first is statistical – comparing your performance data to others – and the other is the process or best practices that make others superior. Both are important.

Identify Opportunities for Improvement

804 Managers should be constantly on the lookout for opportunities to improve performance. More of these can be found by involving the employees themselves. Sometimes an extra shot in the arm can be gained by looking outside of the work area in which the task or process is being performed. Typical areas for comparative performance evaluation include:

✓ customer complaints levels
✓ product or service quality
✓ sales and market share
✓ fixed (overhead) and variable (labor and materials) costs
✓ processing time
✓ response time

805 Choose processes or tasks for benchmarking that are amenable to quantitative as well as qualitative measurement – otherwise you may waste a lot of time unnecessarily.

Your second task is to identify, based on the measured areas, what kind of information you will need to amass. Some examples are

✓ level of quality control
✓ efficiency in production and distribution
✓ workplace safety
✓ employee morale

Plan Your Data Collection

806 Think before you act. Some questions you need answers to include:

✓ How do you go about collecting the data you need?

✓ Do you need an ad hoc benchmarking committee or a permanent team?

✓ Who should be involved and at what point of the process?

✓ Should we look inside the organization or outside?

✓ Are there organizations in different industries that may have similar processes but who have interesting and different ways of doing things that may be useful for us?

✓ Where are the best places to gather the information?

807 Structure the team so it brings different perspectives. It should include at least three people and some or all of the following:

✓ senior managers with the power to authorize changes
✓ front-line employee representatives to contribute to both data collection and process changes based on the results
✓ an outside facilitator to ensure objectivity and that the process is followed quickly and effectively

808 Decide on the best way to collect data. This can be achieved by using:

✓ surveys
✓ checklists detailing key activities you are monitoring
✓ impartial observation of workplace behavior (this may require calling in a professional consultant)
✓ telephone and/or e-mail interviews
✓ in-person interviews and observations inside or at another organization

809 Decide on the best, easiest, and least expensive source of useful data and best practices. These will include:

✓ your own organization (internal and external employees, company newsletters, etc.)
✓ current competitors' employees, and your own employees who recently worked for competitors
✓ industry and trade conferences, journals, and other publications
✓ business books and articles published for the trade
✓ site visits

Collect the Information

810 Present your data collection plan to the people who will be impacted to ensure that it covers most of their concerns and incorporates their ideas. Take suggestions and comments as needed. Don't forget to contact sources of information outside of your organization to encourage them to participate. Offer them access to the collected data if necessary.

811 When collecting data, be sure to make note of behaviors and activities (best practices) that produce superior results. These are the practices that will turn your research into performance improvement reality.

812 Put your plan into action efficiently and with a minimum of disruption to routine. If the method of data collection is long-term (for example, weekly departmental checklists), encourage employees to incorporate it into their routine and institute regular meetings of the benchmarking team to collate and evaluate the data.

813 Start planning for change right away, even before the results come in. It is axiomatic that, if you set out to discover problems and inefficiencies, you will find them.

814 Have the team post regular updates on the benchmarking process in company e-mail or on the general bulletin boards to keep associates interested and apprised.

815 Plan the first information session for a week after the final (or first) batch of results are due to come in, and make the date known to all.

Evaluate the Results

816 Have the team collect all the available data and assemble it into tables or graphs. This will allow you to focus quickly on areas of concern and get right to proposing potential solutions.

817 Make sure the breakdown of the data is specific as well as general – there is no use in determining, for example, that your warehouse chronically ships product late if you don't know what product, to whom, when, and why. As well, prepare the data so industry standards are clearly delineated – this is a quick way to determine how far you have to go to improve poor performance.

818 Once you have the data tabulated, do two things: post the results for the employees to see, and start brainstorming solutions to whatever shortfalls you have discovered. That way, when you have your first information session, you will be armed with solutions but flexible enough to incorporate suggestions from those at the meeting.

819 After the first information session, regroup your team, hammer out the final plans for change, and present them at a staff meeting.

820 Make sure responsibility for implementing these changes is clearly assigned at the meeting.

821 Specify a certain period of time after which you expect the shortfall to be turned around based on the solutions you have presented. This could be as long as one or two years, or as short as a month.

822 Do not stop collecting data. Make it an ongoing process. You will need information to continue the benchmarking cycle and improvement cycle.

Measure the Outcome

823 Continue collecting data on the areas you have identified up until the deadline for the turnaround. Then, look again at the most recent data and determine the success or failure of your plans. Based on this evaluation (it should probably be done in conjunction with the team, and incorporated into a staff meeting), identify new areas needing improvement or new solutions to persistent problem areas.

824 If necessary, alter the membership of the benchmark team to reflect changes in focus. Now repeat the cycle.

How to...
Work with consultants who have not met expectations

I am a little concerned that some of the measures that are proposed may simply increase the number of consultants who are telling businesses what they already know.

— ALASDAIR MORGAN

*F*or one reason or another, *most consulting assignments start with great excitement and hoopla. But few fulfill their promise. And, despite your best efforts, there may be occasions when you feel your money was not well spent and time was wasted. You will know you have made a poor investment if:*

- *The internal clients considered the changes a waste of time.*

- *You paid a premium price for a poor product/process.*

- *The consultant's conduct was unprofessional and resulted in complaints.*

- *Promised deliverables did not materialize in part or in whole.*

Here are some follow-up techniques that can minimize the impact of costly consulting mistakes:

825 Negotiate for a reduced fee for the work already done.

826 Negotiate for reduced fees for upcoming initiatives.

827 Ask the consultant to prepare a recovery strategy at no extra cost.

828 Ask the consultant to give some value-added service, such as training, at little or no cost.

829 Apologize to employees for any mistakes made by the consultant. Make it clear that this is not the company way.

830 If you generally like the services of the consulting firm, but are disappointed with one specific individual, ask for a replacement for the rest of the project.

831 Conduct follow-up research so you are not reacting to opinions expressed by only a few malcontents.

832 If initial reviews for long-term projects are poor, pay a penalty fee to discontinue the initiative rather than hoping for the best.

833 Use every poor consulting experience as an opportunity to understand your role in setting realistic expectations.

834 Consultants have rights too. It is difficult for them to provide appropriate service when companies don't deliver promised information or access to background material. Changing delivery dates, canceling meetings, or delaying payments are unprofessional and are behaviors you would never tolerate in a consultant.

How to...
Work in a virtual environment

Coming together is a beginning.
Keeping together is progress.
Working together is success.

– HENRY FORD

*T*he economy has become *globalized over the last couple of decades as more and more barriers to international trade are removed. In a global economy, people anywhere in the world are able to work on common projects almost as effectively as if they were co-located. And, some of these people work for the same organization while others are consultants or sub-contractors whose involvement is short term. All should be seen as partners in the process.*

While technologies are making it easier to communicate, there is still no substitute for personal contact. So, when the stakes are high and the projects large, there is often an advantage to getting people together at the beginning of a project so they can get to understand and appreciate each other.

Here are some ideas for working effectively together:

835 Choose your team right. Not everyone can work effectively in a virtual team. The best team members are self-directed and able to work independently. They also have a track record of working collaboratively with others in different parts of the world and from different cultural backgrounds.

836 Start off right. The success of a new virtual team will largely be influenced by how they start off. In an ideal world, an important task force should get together physically at the outset if possible so they can

- ✓ learn about and appreciate each other's skill set
- ✓ agree on the goals and deliverables
- ✓ buy in to the time lines
- ✓ create agreed-on performance standard and communication guidelines
- ✓ develop a level of trust among themselves

837 Virtual teams are subject to many of the principles that will ensure the success of regular teams except for the fact that they have less ability to communicate face to face and quickly resolve issues as they arise. Because they need to resort to more impersonal technologies, misunderstandings can easily arise. Some of the primary methods of communication include:

- ✓ *Voice mail.* Set up a system to allow people to call their results in to a central number. This data can be updated regularly and fed back to all interested parties.

- ✓ *Teleconferencing.* The cost of meeting with people out of town is high, so teleconferencing has become the cheaper alternative. It is possible to set up a number and have all members of the meeting call in at a specified time.

- ✓ *Internet Meetings.* It has become increasingly popular to hold meetings and share data on the Internet. New programs are springing up daily that allow people anywhere with Internet access to see each other, share data, and allow for voice exchanges as well as typed messages. It is also possible to share ideas using a whiteboard and have the others exchange ideas in real time.

- ✓ *E-mail.* This has largely taken the place of conventional mail as the best, fastest, and cheapest communication.

E-mail saves paper and stamps, is typically easy to do, and can be sent with attachments, including voice messages.

✓ *Smart phones.* New technologies are enabling people to stay in touch anywhere using SMS, Twitter, and other instant messaging techniques. Within a country, it is easy and inexpensive to update people on a daily basis.

✓ *Chat-lines on the Internet or an Intranet.* Organiza-tions can encourage communications by setting up bulletin boards where people post questions and get answers. Useful information for others on the team can be posted there too.

✓ *Project management.* People sharing the same software can track their progress simultaneously to ensure that they are on time and within budget.

838 Working with people from different cultures in different parts of the world can be challenging. Don't hesitate to pick up the phone if the reaction you're getting from an electronic message is not what was expected. Or, consult others from a similar background who may understand the issue better and be able to guide you toward a constructive resolution.

839 Make people feel like a team. Celebrate small achievements as they occur, especially those that demonstrate the effectiveness of the team.

840 Working with intact co-located teams is difficult enough, so working in a virtual environment requires extra effort and sensitivity. Keep your finger on the pulse and take corrective action any time you feel performance is declining.

How to...
Navigate the compensation and benefits minefield

Money is better than poverty, if only for financial reasons.

– Woody Allen

*T*he governance model requires *that we move away from oligarchic corporate structures. These fiefdoms often enable egotistical, greedy CEOs to lose touch with people on the front line while creating featherbeds for themselves – sometimes translating into compensation packages that are two hundred to five hundred times as much as those of their front-line workers.*

As a leader, you understand that the salaries and benefits you give your people send a message about how much you value them. If you truly believe that people are your most important resource and that the talents of most people are underutilized, you need to compensate them accordingly.

Paying money to employees may not be sufficient to buy their love or loyalty, but it is clearly necessary to attract, motivate, and retain talent. While inadequate compensation is something that may cause some dissatisfaction, few people leave an organization because of the pay. More often they leave because of a poor relationship with their immediate boss. As a leader, your task is not to design the compensation and benefits plan but to provide the philosophy and guiding principles that will influence its design.

In designing or revising a compensation and benefits plan for employees, leaders should ask themselves these tough questions:

841 Who are our employees? Are they people who have worked only in the era of daily downsizing, reorganization, and "rightsizing," making them skeptical of management's long-term plans? Do they see themselves more as free agents, motivated by short-term rewards and opportunities for advancement and learning rather than long-term pension benefits? A more mature and stable workforce will appreciate and value longer-term benefits, whereas younger, more transient workers may be motivated by immediate rewards. The same goes for benefits such as paid holidays, access to gymnasiums, day care, medical benefits, and pensions. Younger people may enjoy benefits such as longer holidays and subsidized health and fitness programs, whereas older workers may prefer better pension and retirement programs.

842 What does the future hold for our business? Are you in a steady industry that rolls along year after year and values long-term retention of people? Or are you in an industry where time horizons are short, technology changes daily, and people do not expect to stay long in their jobs? If that is so, then short-term incentives would be better than long-term rewards.

843 What are our values? Ensure that your compensation systems are aligned with your values by asking yourself questions such as:

✓ What kinds are behaviors are you trying to encourage?

✓ Do you value risk taking or stability?

✓ Does your plan reflect those values?

✓ Is your existing plan compatible with the values that your senior leadership team espouses? If not, consider revision based on your ability to fund that change.

If your values place a great emphasis on building and retaining intellectual capital, then design a program that will give rewards in the longer term. If, on the other hand, your business horizons are shorter, adjust the rewards structure so people will see benefits earlier.

844 Do we need to give incentives? There are many different compensation schemes: base pay, variable pay schemes (bonuses or incentives in addition to base pay), and so on. The philosophy behind each scheme is different. Compensation must always be tailored to the respective business needs and prevailing local market conditions. Compensate in a way that supports the goals of your organization and reinforces what you want your employees to achieve. If incentives are important, ask yourself whether your base pay reflects average performance – that is, showing up for work and doing the job as expected. If superior performance is important, have you given employees an opportunity to share in the rewards (and risks) if targets are exceeded?

845 What is the norm in our industry? Subscribe to industry salary surveys. Share generalities of the information with employees so they become knowledgeable and understand that your salary calculations are not pulled out of the air. Beware of being too specific in case you are unable to pay industry averages, as this will lead to serious discontent. Do everything you can to ensure that non-monetary satisfiers make employees feel management cares about them in other ways.

846 Design your program to reflect the needs of your employees, your industry, and your values.

✓ If your philosophy is to encourage a collaborative environment, ensure that some percentage of the rewards employees receive is based on the performance of their team or department as opposed to individual rewards. Consider a gain-sharing program so all employees can benefit from improvements in productivity or profits.

✓ If bonuses are paid, ensure that employees understand

why and what their role was in achieving the additional pay. Set clear goals and expectations around the portion of compensation that is "variable." Employees should be rewarded based on measures they can influence through their efforts and authority. There is nothing worse than dangling a carrot that is neither realistic nor achievable.

✓ Consider share options or stock ownership for senior employees, if the market climate is such that the shares are likely to steadily increase in value.

847 Be fair. Treat people equally. Make every effort to pay equally for work of comparable value. Consider using a job evaluation system that will help you establish a value for the many different types of jobs in your organization. Such a system will help you determine the value of a job in terms of both internal equity and market comparison. Then communicate, communicate, communicate so everyone understands the system.

848 Be sure to distinguish between salaries/benefits and recognition. The latter consists of one-time rewards for specific achievements that may or may not be repeated, whereas salaries and benefits represent the leaders' obligations to take care of the basic needs of employees. They are unrelated to motivation.

849 If recognition is not separated psychologically from compensation, employees will expect it to be repeated. They will become discouraged if similar achievements are not acknowledged in a similar fashion. In fact, it is advisable to recognize individual efforts in non-monetary ways with anything from a sincere thank-you to token gifts, meals, and the like.

850 Give the best benefits you can afford. Good benefits are expected as part of a compensation package and are rarely considered a motivator although they may be considered a value that might prevent someone from "jumping ship." They may not give a significant competitive advantage in attracting top talent, but providing good benefits demonstrates that you care. A system of optional benefits to suit your people is a smart way to go. These benefits can range from health and dental plans, to paid leave, flextime, and subsidized day care and cafeteria, to generous vacations and sports club memberships. What you provide should be consistent with what you and your organization value and with the interests of your employees.

851 Communicate your compensation and benefit plan in as many ways as possible, because misunderstandings are likely to occur. Hold meetings to share the information, especially if it is complicated or offers the employee many options, and supplement the information with easy-to-understand documentation.

852 Be cautious when changing the structure of your compensation and benefits program. Making changes can create a minefield. Expect to get few accolades for improvements and significant negativity about real or perceived cutbacks. Hence the need to communicate openly, honestly, and frequently is critical when any changes to compensation are made. It is vital to listen and respond to concerns and questions.

How to...
Improve your corporate governance and transparency

Even in a time of elephantine vanity and greed, one never has to look far to see the campfires of gentle people.

– GARRISON KEILLOR

In **the light of** *an alarming number of high-profile cases of theft, greed, and misuse of corporate assets, directors and senior corporate leaders are being pushed into drastically changing the way organizational assets are taken care of. This process is known as governance.*

Governance is about how easily stakeholders can exert influence and track the affairs and direction of an organization. It reflects their interests, how their views are included in decisions, how decisions are made, and how the decision makers are held accountable.

Governance is not about restrictions. It is more about creating democratic processes in organizations to enable and encourage freedom of initiative and enterprise. This freedom is designed to build trust between all the stakeholders so they can focus on their goals, create world-class products and services, and optimize financial benefits for shareholders and employees.

Improving governance requires that we strengthen and change the nature of the relationships between stakeholders. And it starts at the top, with the relationship between the board and the operating organization. It requires that the board use

increased power to ensure compliance of the officers of the orga-
nization to all standards set by government and other outside
regulatory bodies.

Legislation alone will not lead to significant improvements in
governance. The attitude of senior management is key.

853 Openness, transparency and good governance is the responsibility of all executives and the board, but managers have
their part to play too.

854 Good governance will enhance the performance of an organization if the executive team:

- ✓ takes a longer-term focus on financial performance
  beyond quarterly results
- ✓ establishes strong boards that are independent of those
  running the daily affairs of the organization
- ✓ establishes methods for listening to the shareholders and
  staff and responding to their needs
- ✓ ensures that it does not become ensnarled in defensive
  activities that detract from management's ability to take
  risks
- ✓ promotes strategic planning and the execution of those
  plans
- ✓ emphasizes and promotes success instead of avoiding
  failure

855 At the heart of good governance is accountability. The benefits of increased accountability include:

- ✓ increased employee confidence in the organization
- ✓ more effective use of assets
- ✓ greater debate within an organization as to how better to
  allocate resources to competing priorities. The creativity
  that flows from this debate will lead to improved
  performance
- ✓ increased participation by venture capitalists willing to
  contribute knowledge capital, as well as financial capital,
  to boost shareholder value

856 Good governance is characterized by

✓ *Involvement.* Everyone is capable of being heard.

✓ *Transparency.* Information is available to all.

✓ *Consensus decisions.* Attempts are made, when practical, to achieve broad agreement to decisions.

✓ *Equity.* All people, no matter what race, color, creed, gender, or sexual orientation, have an equal ability to participate.

✓ *Effectiveness.* The organization's resources are utilized effectively.

✓ *Strategic vision.* There is agreement about the general direction the organization is taking.

✓ *Accountability.* Decision makers are responsible for their behavior.

857 Good governance requires that the board and the CEO become independent of one another so as to prevent collusion. Ideally,

✓ the CEO will be a non-voting member of the board

✓ in strategy formulation and policymaking, the CEO will be seen as a full partner with the board

✓ the board will focus on monitoring performance rather than formulating policies

✓ the CEO will attend all board meetings and participate fully in all discussions

✓ in large organizations, the board will monitor performance through standing committees, including an audit body

858 The board does not involve itself in the day-to-day running of the organization – that is the task of the CEO and their management team. The primary tasks of the board are to

✓ create a strategic plan, which sets the course for the organization

✓ regularly update the strategic plan as circumstances change

✓ set the organization's direction, ensuring that it has a compelling vision and mission

✓ develop clear objectives stemming from the mission

✓ create a set of values that will enable the corporation to operate effectively and professionally

✓ see to it that the assets of the corporation are being effectively utilized

859 Good governance often means change. Here are some specific actions that may demonstrate an organization's good intentions.

✓ Increase the number of independent directors to the point where they form a majority on the board. Size matters, and the numbers of the board will depend on the nature of the organization and the complexity of its operations. As a general guide, however, the board should be made up of between five and seven members.

✓ Ensure that all committee members are non-management so decision making is impartial

✓ Conduct some board meetings without management present, ensuring open and candid discussions

✓ Promote stock ownership (in the case of for-profit companies) so directors have a stake in the long-term success of the organization

✓ Seek shareholder approval for significant change in systems of compensation for senior executives

✓ Promote the concept of pay-for-performance rather than stock option. Rather, bonuses and "performance share units" should be linked to specific performance objectives – cash-flow, profits, or customer satisfaction – rather than stock price.

✓ Seek third-party professional advice when reviewing and evaluating compensation practices

✓ Separate the role of chairperson of the board from those of president and CEO. The chairperson should be seen as the chief governance officer.

✓ Separate the audit and risk management committees to recognize the importance and contribution of each. These committees should be viewed as committees of the board, not autonomous entities.

✓ Design compensation plans for executives that are aligned with corporate strategy rather than with short-term share value increases.

✓ Enhance the competence of directors by creating position descriptions for the chairs of each committee and the chairperson of the board. Then – scary as this may be – have each director assess themselves and each other. When shortcomings are identified, have each person develop a plan for improvement. Any director refusing to improve should be removed.

How to...
Create a mission and vision

Keep your dreams alive. Understand to achieve anything requires faith and belief in yourself, vision, hard work, determination, and dedication. Remember all things are possible for those who believe.

– GAIL DEVERS

*E**very organization** needs a mission. It gives a daily reminder and focus for all stakeholders about what needs to be done. Unfortunately, many organizations take weeks, months, and even years to develop a mission. And, having done so, the mission is seldom referred to as a guide for daily actions making the exercise a waste of time and effort.*

Using a simple process you will be able to create a compelling vision and mission and also integrate it into the operating fabric of your organization. A vision is a short statement that is engaging and compelling and talks about the future state of the organization. A mission is more pragmatic and speaks to the daily deliverables to all stakeholders in the organization's ideal state.

The following steps will make the process easy to follow and would apply especially in organizations that have a mission but could benefit from creating missions for each department thereby building higher accountability, ownership, and performance.

Preliminary Meeting

860 Hold a meeting with your staff at which time you

- ✓ inform them of the value of having a mission
- ✓ explain what a mission is
- ✓ invite them to participate in developing a mission
- ✓ show them how it will be done and what it should contain
- ✓ show them examples of missions

861 Form a subcommittee to do the detail work, if your work area is large. If you have fewer than a dozen people, involve them all.

862 There are many ways to create a vision statement. An interesting and enjoyable process is beginning by getting together as a group and asking each person to create their own vision. How?

- ✓ Each is given a piece of paper and some crayons. They are instructed to imagine they are a three-year-old child and to then draw a picture of the organization as it may be five to ten years hence through the eyes of a child. Why a child? Children are very creative and have no inhibitions or hesitations when asked to draw.

- ✓ After three or four minutes, ask each person to describe key aspects of their drawing. Expect many examples of stick people with smiling faces, holding hands, standing in a circle, and the sun shining and other metaphors for growth and success. These key ideas can then be given to a smaller team to craft a statement that reflects the emotions created through the drawing exercise.

- ✓ Bring drafts back to the bigger group for their fine-tuning and ultimate endorsement.

863 The process of creating a mission statement is a little different. It needs more structure. Before your design meeting, have everyone complete their own mission statement by answering the questions:

✓ WHO are we? State the name of the organization, work area, or team.

✓ WHAT do we do? Briefly state the nature of the product or service you give.

✓ HOW do we do it? Describe what you do in terms of categories such as quality, responsiveness, service, cost effectiveness, or any other dimensions you have control of.

✓ For WHOM do we do it? Describe your customers.

✓ WHERE do we do it? Describe the geographical territory you cover.

✓ WHY do we do it? Describe the benefits to the internal stakeholders, the shareholders, and staff.

Once they have incorporated all the elements, have each person combine their thoughts into one or two sentences.

Decision Meeting

864 Conduct a meeting to construct the mission.

✓ Have each participant write their statement on a piece of flip-chart paper and post these around the room.

✓ Get the feedback on each statement in turn, identifying the strengths and positives in each.

✓ Underline useful ideas from each.

✓ Take the best ideas from each statement.

✓ Write the ideas on a whiteboard. This will allow you to change and modify ideas, words, and sentence structure with ease.

✓ Continue wordsmithing the mission until everyone is satisfied. This should not take more than one or two hours.

After the Meeting

865 Circulate the mission to people who were not present. Ask for their feedback.

866 Ensure that the mission is aligned with the vision.

867 Hold a final short meeting to add any minor finishing touches to the mission.

868 Post the mission in the workplace.

869 Have all staff commit to the mission and vision by signing each statement.

870 Post the mission in your meeting room to ensure that the mission has a direct bearing on all team activities.

871 Identify ways of measuring the extent to which you are meeting your mission or not. Post graphs of these indicators where everyone can see them and follow the trends.

872 Celebrate your area's progress in meeting its mission. When indicators of performance decline are evident, involve your people in finding new ways to improve.

How to...
Plan strategically

*Let's talk about the future because that's
where we're going to spend most of our time.*

– JACK WELCH

*Strategic planning is an activity usually considered to be the
domain of senior managers. But all managers need to think and
act strategically so they can influence the future rather than be
influenced by it. The steps you must take to develop a plan are set
out below. Customize them to suit your work environment.*

Plan to Plan

873 Strategic planning is a slow, difficult process. You need to
consider how to develop the plan to avoid having to retrace
steps and fill in gaps later. So, before the journey begins,
consider:

✓ how much time you and your team can devote to the
process including research and documentation. The
answer will influence how extensively you want to
research all the options the first time around.

✓ what support you will need to call on from those who will
need to contribute

✓ to what extent you can involve the people who must help
you implement changes

✓ what steps in the process you will take, based on your

time and resource availability
- ✓ your deadline for completing the plan
- ✓ how you will ensure that the process brings about significant value-added changes in performance rather than remaining an interesting exercise

Assemble the Team

874 Create a team of people, of between four to eight people who

- ✓ represent a good cross section of the organization
- ✓ are eager to participate
- ✓ have complementary skills, experiences, and perspectives

Take an Inward Look at Yourself

875 Before looking to the future, take a look at yourself. Conduct a study to highlight what you do well and what you could do better – your strengths and weaknesses. This study must cover all stakeholders the most important of whom are your employees and clients/customers/patients/taxpayers.

- ✓ Look at your operating statistics to evaluate your costs, quality, responsiveness, morale, and health and safety issues.

- ✓ Conduct surveys, interviews, or focus groups to establish as much empirical information as possible.

- ✓ Benchmark your performance with others inside and outside of your industry so you have a comparison between your performance and that of others around you. This will help you develop a sense of how effective your services and processes are. Your research should, as a minimum, establish

  - the level of engagement of your employees
  - what makes them happy and what management practices cause morale to decline
  - why people leave the organization

- the primary causes of grievances and absenteeism
- how effective your customer service is
- why customers leave you
- what attracted new customers

Look to the Future: Develop a Vision

876 Think about the future. What do you see? More importantly, what are you going to work toward? Create a vision statement. The vision represents what you aspire to become. A vision statement is typically a short one-line statement that represents the dreams and aspirations of the leadership team. The statement may not be entirely possible or practical, but it will serve to energize the employees who will share the responsibility for working toward it. Words such as "world leader," "the benchmark," "world class," and "most respected" are appropriate in the vision.

Describe Your Daily Actions: Develop a Mission Statement

877 Create a mission statement that clearly describes how you will satisfy your stakeholders each day. Your mission should be

✓ easily understood
✓ short – not longer than two or three sentences
✓ fairly specific, so it can prompt goal setting and tracking
✓ general enough so it will not date
✓ something employees feel good about
✓ posted in a prominent place, with all staff members' signatures, to confirm their agreement

Build a Model for Success

878 Based on your research and your aspirations for the future, create a model for success. The critical elements may include

- ✓ leadership development and succession planning
- ✓ deployments of key performance indicators for all teams and departments
- ✓ a culture of innovation and creativity
- ✓ a system of performance management with goals, recognition, and rewards
- ✓ the establishment of best practices, service standards, and documented processes wherever possible

Set Goals for Major Strategic Changes

879 Describe the major changes that must take place and dates when these will be complete.

Create Objectives for the Next Financial Year

880 For each of the major objectives described above, create goals that need to be achieved in the next twelve months. These need to be

- ✓ **S** pecific
- ✓ **M** easurable
- ✓ **A** greed upon
- ✓ **R** ealistic
- ✓ **T** ime bound

881 Assign responsibility to individuals for implementation. Ensure that there is at least one Key Performance Indicator attached to the attainment of the objective so it can be measured and tracked and that those undertaking the changes can be held accountable and rewarded for their efforts.

- ✓ Manage the changes.
- ✓ Encourage change and action by posting plans and measures prominently.
- ✓ Follow up to show your interest in strategic initiatives.

✓ Help remove roadblocks and encourage the removal of resistance or falling back to the old ways.

✓ Celebrate achievements, no matter how small.

✓ Post plans in your work area so everyone is aware of them. Delete each item as it is dealt with.

✓ Create a list of obstacles that will prevent you from meeting your goals. Prioritize them. Categorize those you have control over and those you don't. Focus on key roadblocks that you do control. Develop specific actions to deal with them.

Scan the Environment

882 On an ongoing basis, look outside your organization for trends and changes that may impact you or that you may take advantage of. This can be done by

✓ circulating articles of interest
✓ subscribing to and circulating trade journals
✓ attending conferences
✓ visiting trade shows
✓ visiting competitors
✓ visiting customers

Make the Process Ongoing

883 Review and adjust your plans regularly so the plan becomes a living process and not a periodic exercise brought on by a crisis.

As Henry R. Luce put it, "Business, more than any other occupation, is a continual dealing with the future: it is a continual calculation, an instinctive exercise in foresight."

How to...
Create a partnership relationship with your union

History is a great teacher. Now everyone knows that the labor movement did not diminish the strength of the nation but enlarged it. By raising the living standards of millions, labor miraculously created a market for industry and lifted the whole nation to undreamed of levels of production. Those who attack labor forget these simple truths, but history remembers them.

– Martin Luther King Jr.

Unions are an important part of our labor and employment structure. They protect workers from unfair treatment and exploitation. While their influence has been in steady decline over the past half century, it is critical for leaders to manage their relationship with unionized staff effectively to ensure they are contributing, engaged, and productive. Failure to do so can result in unnecessary grievances, work stoppages, and strikes. Here are some daily strategies that make for productive relationships:

884 Come to terms with the fact that your employees are unionized. It is unlikely that the bargaining unit will become decertified, so learn to manage the relationship to the advantage of all concerned.

885 Treat union people as part of the family, not as the enemy. Think of them as customers. People will respond positively to a constructive and open work environment.

886 Treat union representatives as your peers and partners and they, in turn, are less likely to treat you as a foe. Your relationship must be constantly nurtured – trust takes a long time to build.

887 Be prepared for ups and downs in the relationship with your union representative. However, if you consider the union a legitimate partner, the ups will be greater than the downs, and you will be able to count on its cooperation more often than not.

888 Understand the differences between the union's objectives and those of your organization, but look for common goals to build on. Make sure new initiatives benefit everyone and do not infringe on your collective agreement. If changes could conflict with the agreement, work with your union representatives to resolve the issue with a win-win outcome.

889 Review your contract thoroughly. Consult your labor relations expert if you have difficulty interpreting it.

890 Train all managers to understand and work within the letter and spirit of the collective agreement.

891 Respect your contract: It was negotiated in good faith. Learn to live with what you have negotiated.

892 Be careful about bending rules. Bending rules establishes precedents that the union could seek to perpetuate. Do so only if there is agreement on the part of the union that this will be an exception, not the rule.

893 Make sure your leadership style is based on fairness, integrity, and consistency.

894 Monitor the relationship and measure its effectiveness in terms of grievances, work stoppages, absenteeism, and productivity. If these indicators suggest a problem – high grievances are a clear indicator of unaddressed issues – identify root causes and develop solutions.

895 Meet regularly with your shop stewards and representatives in a cordial climate with the objective of relationship building, strengthening trust, and sharing information. Your behavior at these encounters should demonstrate a sincere willingness to cooperate.

896 Keep your shop stewards and union representatives informed of all issues that could impact their members. The more open you are, the easier it will be for you to avoid a negative grapevine.

897 If your organization needs significant changes in the next contract, work with your union representatives to prepare them and the membership for the new ideas. You can do this by

- ✓ sharing your thinking regularly so new ideas do not come as a surprise later on
- ✓ giving people articles describing how other organizations have managed similar changes successfully
- ✓ visiting organizations in which dramatic change has been accomplished to see how it has impacted their people. You can then avoid their mistakes.

VIII

How to...
TAKE CARE
OF YOURSELF

Lessons 898–970

How to...
Set and achieve personal objectives

You've removed most of the roadblocks to success when you've learned the difference between motion and direction.

– BILL COPELAND

*I*magine *going hiking in the bush without a compass or a map. Sure, it's fun for a while – you feel adventurous and daring – but, sooner or later you will get lost. Now imagine pursuing your career without clearly articulated goals.*

What should your goals be, and how should you go about getting them?

898 Make goals and objectives a part of who you are. Why? Goals are compatible with your beliefs, and in turn, define you.

899 You have your mirror so you can check your appearance before going to work. Similarly, put your goals in a visible place so you can check them every morning.

900 If you look at your goals every day, you will soon notice if one of them seems a bit off. This may happen because your values have slowly shifted.

901 Goals should also be prioritized with respect to your values.

For example, if you enjoy volunteer work at a homeless shelter, arrange your schedule so you work less overtime.

902 Goals can be short, medium, or long-term projects. The more immediate the goal, the more disciplined you need to be to get it done.

903 Break down long-term goals into yearly, monthly, or daily steps – earning a million dollars before you reach a given age is much easier to achieve when you know what each month's contribution should be.

904 Increase your sense of personal responsibility by telling all those closest to you about your goals. The more people you tell, the more you will be reminded of them.

905 Arrange a mutual watchdog plan: help someone else stick to their goals, while they keep you to yours.

906 As stated above, be SMART. Use this simple formula to articulate your objectives:

✓ **S** is for specific. Give a number or a name to your goal. If you want to be senior vice-president of marketing in five years, say that, rather than, "I want to make senior-level management at some point."

✓ **M** is for measurable. This goes with specific. You shouldn't be able to fudge whether you have succeeded or failed. If you put a number to your goal, you'll know whether you've reached it.

✓ **A** is for agreed-upon. Be willing to negotiate the goal if others are involved. Their input will lead to additional commitment.

✓ **R** is for realistic. Don't plan to be the head of the NATO if you're not going to join the army.

✓ **T** is for time-based. Break the goals down into time-bits, and measure what you've achieved in each time-bit. The best way to have a measurable goal is to give yourself a final deadline, then break the goal down into smaller time-based steps.

How to...
Deal with adversity

Every great achievement was first impossible.

– GUY CLARKE

Life is full of twists and turns. And organizations need to withstand regular bumps in the road. Some challenges are easy to solve and short lived while others require a more drastic dose of medicine. These setbacks will test your mettle as a leader because employees will be looking to you for guidance or reassurance that they are doing the right thing.

907 Manage the grapevine! If employees suspect there is problem but don't know the details, they will usually assume the worst. They will anticipate a problem if

- ✓ regular meetings are cancelled
- ✓ their managers disappear into meetings off site or behind closed doors
- ✓ no one is saying anything about the current state of business but overtime has been cancelled, people are laid off unexpectedly, or a major contract has been lost

908 If there is no explanation from leadership, rumors will start to fly. And they are unlikely to be positive.

909 Be honest and forthright in your communications. Hold information meetings with as many of the employees as possible, so everyone gets the same message at the same time. Be as honest and frank as possible. At the same time, point to the positive outcomes that are likely to result from difficult and sometimes unpopular decisions.

910 Engage employees whenever possible. Meet with them frequently to solicit their input. The more the employees are involved in finding solutions, the greater will be their buy-in and commitment.

911 Create task forces to deal with systemic challenges. Utilize the talents of your high-potentials, showing confidence in them. This will reduce the possibility of losing some of your valued up-and-coming talent.

912 Listen to employees and understand their concerns. Listening means more than simply hearing their words. Listen to what they are feeling. Respond to the fears and anxieties you detect in their body language, not only to what they tell you.

913 Create an environment in which the criteria for success are known. Promote certainty so people know the goals, the limits of their decision making, and the guidelines by which they are expected to make those decisions. These steps will help remove uncertainties that eat away at superior performance.

914 Demonstrate sacrifice. Be the first to volunteer for longer work hours or reduced pay.

915 If layoffs are necessary, handle the process as humanely as possible. Treat people with dignity, so they leave on as positive a note as possible.

916 Deal with the aftermath of a layoff. Don't ignore the feelings – such as guilt – of the people left behind. Acknowledge those feelings and help people move forward. Review the new business model with them so they become more confident in the future of the organization.

How to...
Manage your career

Each of us has special talents.
It's our duty to make the most of them.

– ROBERT E. ALLEN

*L*oyalty to organizations *has faded fast because organizations have shown little loyalty to employees. Being laid off no longer comes with a sense of shame. It is now commonplace and no longer associated with ineptitude. Research indicates that career executives are spending less time than ever in jobs before moving on to – hopefully – bigger and better positions. This creates many more opportunities for ambitious and smart people than ever before. You always need to be ready to make the next move or to be invited to undertake a more advanced, high-profile challenge.*

917 Taking care of the stakeholders is important, but consider yourself number one. Every leader needs to set aside time for personal development. You must be able to land on your feet if your career suddenly hits a roadblock – or a superhighway.

918 Stay in line management – that's where the action is! Line managers are in the limelight. They produce the crucial results in sales and production. Staff positions are important, but they serve the people who serve the key stakeholders – the customers.

919 Take responsibility for your career. Don't expect your boss to advocate for you or promote you. You need to plan your own career path, determine the knowledge and level of performance that will take you there, and acquire and demonstrate the leadership competencies that are defined in your organization.

920 Set goals for yourself. Decide where you'd like to be three, five, and ten years from now. Make a list of obstacles that might prevent you from achieving those goals. Then identify the roadblocks and what you can do to remove them. Don't get overwhelmed if the obstacles look daunting. Develop plans to systematically remove them, one at a time, over time.

921 Be your customers' best friend. Your customers are key stakeholders and they, more than anyone, will sell your skills to the top decision makers. So identify the highest-profile customers and do everything you can to ensure they sing your praises.

922 Think strategically about the future of your organization and your career. Review it at least once per month, as circumstances can change quickly. Consider new developments in your organization and in your current industry. How will these affect you? What opportunities do they create? What challenges do they present?

923 Become your own greatest advocate. Look at yourself as a client who needs PR. Make yourself known. Make sure that people in your industry know about you and your accomplishments. At corporate and industry gatherings, stay around so you can network, looking particularly for the movers and shakers who can influence your career.

924 Be ready to take advantage of new opportunities when they occur. They will probably happen when you least expect it.

Realize that the job you have will not last forever. Chances are that, sooner or later, you will either be offered a promotion, perhaps the job of your dreams – or be given an awkward handshake and asked to leave right away.

925 Take care of yourself. Keep your mind and body in good shape. Keeping fit will make you feel good, look good, and carry yourself with enthusiasm and confidence. And if you smoke, make the extra effort to kick the habit as smokers are becoming the pariahs of society.

926 Treat everyone with respect. Never do anything that could embarrass a peer, boss, or member of the board. Deal with disagreements in private. If you need to challenge someone, ensure that you focus on the issue and not the person. Recognize that their position is legitimate, even though you may see things differently.

927 Develop alliances. Identify people who might want to hold you back, and be careful not to offend them. Better still, ensure good relations with their subordinates. If someone belittles you behind your back, others will speak up in your defense and the person who is showing no class will harm their own reputation as a consequence.

928 Be nice to people. Get to know as many of your colleagues by name as possible. When you have time, practice management by walking around. In fact, make a point of setting aside time to get as friendly with as many people as possible.

929 Go the extra mile. Be a little better than your peers. Come early to meetings. Stay an extra five minutes before taking lunch or going home. Put in extra time when a situation demands it – without sacrificing too much family time.

930 Don't take work home unless absolutely necessary. If you have a heavy workload, close your door to make sure that you focus and clean your desk before going home. A healthy and happy home life will enable you to be positive and enthusiastic at work.

931 Take a leadership role in the most important and visible projects. Focus on them and make sure they are completed on time and on budget.

932 Be obliging, especially if the CEO or your board has a request. This will earn you a can-do reputation, which will position you well for promotion.

933 Don't surprise your boss – they hate that! Bosses like advance notice of new initiatives that will require some thought before action is needed. If one of your projects is going off the rails, let your boss know as soon as possible – before they hear the bad news through the grapevine.

934 Make your boss look good, especially if they are the president! This will pay huge dividends sooner or later. And if you can, make your boss's boss look even better. That person will have even more influence over your career. Why? Your boss may feel threatened by the possibility of being replaced by you, but your boss's boss certainly won't.

935 If you are frustrated with your role in the organization, consider the fit between your skills and your job. Would other roles suit you better and allow you to shine? If so, how?

936 Don't quit! Let your boss know you're frustrated. Be specific as to why, but be careful not to blame them in any way. Ask them for advice as to how you might resolve the issue.

937 If they agree a new direction would benefit both you and the organization, then the ball is in your court.

938 Take every opportunity to research and discover new

opportunities. Find out about other jobs that may interest you and match your skills. Watch for job postings.

939 Volunteer for task forces that occur in your area of interest. This will expose you to people in that area and give you a better opportunity to understand the issues in more detail.

940 Take every opportunity to learn. Learn from your mistakes, from reading, from a mentor, from listening intently to others, and from taking regular courses. Research new ideas and share them with others too, since nothing will help you internalize new ideas better than teaching others.

How to...
Be a successful protégé

Mentoring is a brain to pick, an ear to listen,
and a push in the right direction.

– John Crosby

*W*hen Ulysses embarked *on his long journey in* The Odyssey, *he chose his wise friend Mentor to guard, guide, and teach his son, Telemachus. All of us can benefit from having someone to help us. But picking the right person is key.*

Not every smart, articulate, experienced person makes for a perfect mentor. Picking, or being matched with the wrong person, will produce limited results. In fact, the outcome could even be a career-limiting experience as your mentor may bad-mouth you in the organization. To the extent that you can choose your mentor, find someone who meets all or most of these criteria:

941 Find the best and most suitable mentor. Don't let your HR department team you up with a mentor without being actively involved in the process. Choose someone who

- ✓ has your admiration
- ✓ has achieved something similar to what you are striving to do
- ✓ would care to spend the time with you
- ✓ is patient, empathetic, and willing to allow you to play a meaningful role in the relationship

942 Finding someone to mentor you successfully can take time. An ideal mentor will be one who

✓ does not work in your department. Find someone who can bring you a new perspective; someone with different technical skills and work experiences.

✓ is more experienced than you. This usually, though not necessarily, goes with age. A person with experience will have moved between jobs, organizations, and industries. They will have a greater variety of experiences. They will have made more mistakes to learn from.

✓ is senior to you in the organization. This will enable them to bring a larger perspective to you, one that often escapes people in the trenches.

✓ is humble. A humble person is not a know-it-all. They are prepared to think before talking. Better still, they would expect you to answer some of your own issues rather than feeding you answers and doing the thinking for you.

✓ facilitates problem solving by acting as a sounding board. Because they are concerned about your growth, they force you to clarify your understanding. When asked for answers, they throw the ball back to you with questions such as "Well, what do you think?" or "What are some of your options?"

✓ thrives on other people's successes. This person cares about you. They celebrate and find joy in your achievements.

943 Ideal mentors are people who

✓ are great role models
✓ listen more than they talk
✓ enjoy learning from their protégés
✓ care about and value the relationship
✓ have a great attitude – positive, upbeat, and optimistic
✓ care about honesty (they know how to give feedback that is frank and focuses on the problem, not your personality)
✓ are tolerant (they accept you for who and what you are without wanting to change you)

944 At your first meeting, come prepared with clear objectives and an agenda. Key items on your agenda should be

- ✓ *Your needs.* Are you looking for help with your career? Developing political savvy? Improving your knowledge about the industry? Make sure your mentor is the best person to help you.

- ✓ *Your expectations of the mentor.* Do you expect your mentor to be a fountain of knowledge, a friend, a sounding board, an advocate, an observer, or some combination of these? Not many people are equally adept at these different roles.

- ✓ *The frequency and length of meetings.* Will the meetings be in person, on the phone, or by Skype? And, will they be held during or after work hours?

- ✓ *Boundaries.* Set up guidelines to clarify the things that are inside or outside the relationship. Issues of confidentiality are important. Also, will you confine yourself to business issues, or can they cover issues outside of work? And what about honesty? How frank will you be with each other if either party does or says something the other considers offensive? How will you deal with these issues?

- ✓ *Length of the relationship.* Most relationships last about a year. What expectations do you both have?

945 The ongoing relationship will be effective if you

- ✓ meet your commitments
- ✓ respect the time of the mentor by attending meetings on time and finishing on time
- ✓ confine yourself mostly to the issues the mentor is best qualified to help you with
- ✓ come prepared. If you have a problem, bring a solution for consideration. The mentor's job is more to act as a sounding board and facilitator rather than to advise you continually.

✓ do not betray confidences of other people to the mentor

✓ show your appreciation to the mentor, particularly if they have gone out on a limb for you or advocated for you in some way

✓ give polite but assertive feedback if you feel the mentor has betrayed your confidence in any way

✓ are not afraid to tell your mentor the relationship is not working for you as a result of a mismatch. It's better to pull the plug or the relationship early on in the process than allow it to continue without either of you getting any benefit.

946 When the relationship is becoming stale and the learning transfer is of limited value, it may be time to call a halt to the meetings or take a break.

✓ Be frank with the mentor. They will probably be grateful.

✓ Show your appreciation. A small gift or a lunch is appropriate. Also, write them a thank-you note outlining what they have done for you.

✓ If you have been part of a formal mentoring program, send a note of appreciation to the program coordinator.

How to...
Deal effectively with stress

The bow too tensely strung is easily broken.

– PUBLILIUS SYRUS

Stress is a major cause of work absenteeism and a host of social problems. Stress is different for each individual. What bothers one person may be brushed off as trivial to another. Similarly, dealing with the issue is different for each individual. Researchers suggest the primary cause of stress in the workplace is having little or no control over one's work life. So many organizations tout the benefit of engagement, but most prevent front line people from even spending thirty dollars on a three-hole punch without approval.

Here are some things you can do to reduce your stress.

947 Accept the fact that stress is a natural part of modern life. Some stress can even be positive, since it increases the body's production of adrenaline, which generates energy.

948 Identify the things you enjoy doing most and that take your mind off stressful situations. Build more of these activities into your daily routine.

949 Break up your working day so you have time to refresh yourself. Make a point of getting away from your desk to clear your head and recharge your batteries.

950 Get as much exercise as possible. The better you feel about your body and the better shape your body is in, the better you will feel mentally.

951 Establish a relationship with a good listener. When you are close to your boiling point, talk through your frustrations with your confidant. Talking will relieve the pressure. Bottling up your problems can cause mental and physical illness.

952 Practice the principle espoused in the Serenity Prayer.

God grant me the serenity to accept the things I cannot change, the courage to change the things I can, and the wisdom to know the difference.

So, don't hang on to issues you can do nothing about. Deal with those aspects that you can change. For example, if you're flying in turbulence and are frightened, there is nothing you can do to control the outside weather conditions. But, you can have a glass or two of wine to help you relax.

953 Find an outside interest or hobby. The time spent on this activity will give you a mental break.

954 Experiment with your diet. Eliminate foods that contain caffeine, as this can increase your tension. Sugar before bed will reduce your ability to sleep.

955 Learn to manage your time better. Constantly fighting the clock is a losing battle. You must change your habits and generate more free time to relax or do the things you want to do.

956 Don't use medication, drugs, or alcohol to ease the problem. These substances temporarily mask the problem without solving it. You must remove the causes of your problem.

957 Meditate once or twice a day, or as needed, for ten to twenty minutes. To achieve this relaxed state:

- ✓ focus on a pleasant image or word
- ✓ close your eyes and lie or sit in a comfortable position
- ✓ consciously relax all your muscles by focusing on each from your head to your toes, allowing your body to "sink"
- ✓ breathe slowly and naturally, maintaining a mental image of a pleasant scene or repeating a key word (mantra) to yourself

Don't worry about perfecting your technique. If it's not working perfectly, refocus and put other thoughts out of your mind.

958 Learn to say no assertively when the demands of others are overloading your time and ability.

959 Delegate more of your workload so you will have more time to think, plan, and prioritize. Typical tasks to delegate include:

- ✓ routine items
- ✓ data collection
- ✓ some meetings

960 Understand your body and mind so you can take action before things get out of hand. Typical symptoms that suggest you're approaching burnout include:

- ✓ becoming preoccupied with your own thoughts when in the company of others, so you find it hard to follow or engage in meaningful discussions
- ✓ having difficulty shaking off minor illnesses such as coughs and colds
- ✓ becoming ill more often than you used to
- ✓ seeing less of your family and friends than you used to
- ✓ becoming increasingly short-tempered with people
- ✓ being more irritable in company than you used be

- ✓ working longer hours but not accomplishing more
- ✓ missing deadlines and appointments without realizing it
- ✓ tiring easily
- ✓ cutting back on recreational activities you usually enjoy

How to...
Become the CEO of your life

Think beyond your lifetime if you want to accomplish something truly worthwhile.

– WALT DISNEY

Our lives *are not a dress rehearsal for something else. This is the real thing, the only chance we get to make the most of our lives. We can never know when the final moment of our lives may occur. So, we need to take every opportunity to make each day count as if it were our last.*

961 Avoid things that add to your stress. Don't obsess over numbers that never help you and that are not critically important to you such as your age, the quality of your car, your height, weight, or earnings.

962 Surround yourself with people who make you feel good. These are friends and family who are happy, smile often, and always see the glass as half full. Let go of the complainers.

963 Keep learning. Learn in formal situations and learn from your mistakes. Seek out people who have complementary skills and ideas. Learn from them. Learn more about computers, crafts, gardening, or whatever may interest you. Never let your enthusiasm die or your brain become idle.

964 Enjoy the simple things. Learn to smell the roses. Appreciate the laughter of kids, the caring of people in love, the beauty of a spectacular sunset, the majesty of the sea, and the beauty of a spiderweb.

965 Laugh often and with gusto. Never feel embarrassed to laugh out loud – it's often infectious. Laugh until you feel as if your body's going to explode. It won't.

966 Deal with grief as a necessary but passing phase that cannot be avoided. But don't get stuck in it. Life is too short. Honor those who have passed, and care for those who are unwell. But move on – don't get stuck in things you have no control over. Treat your tears as a way to help you wash the sadness away. Enjoy the sense of relief and move on.

967 Fill your life with love. Surround yourself with people you love and who love you in return. Listen to music you love, over and over, till it stops giving you enjoyment. Place pictures of the people and things you love where you will see them often.

968 Cherish your health. If it is good, preserve it. If it is unstable, improve it. If it is beyond anything you can do to improve, get help.

969 Avoid feeling guilty. Treat yourself to things that give you plea-sure. Have the occasional piece of chocolate or your favorite full-fat ice cream. And (within reason) buy that luxury item you've always wanted. Savor these times of indulgence, but don't rely on them too often to make you happy.

970 Tell the people you love that you love them – often.

As George Carlin put it, "Life is not measured by the number of breaths we take, but by the moments that take our breath away."

CPSIA information can be obtained
at www.ICGtesting.com
Printed in the USA
BVHW061936110221
599953BV00003B/7